THE UPANISHADS

Breath of the Eternal

D0964067

BOOKS BY SWAMI PRABHAVANANDA

Original Works

THE ETERNAL COMPANION (Brahmananda:
    His Life and Teachings)
THE SERMON ON THE MOUNT ACCORDING
    TO VEDANTA
RELIGION IN PRACTICE
YOGA AND MYSTICISM
THE SPIRITUAL HERITAGE OF INDIA (with
    Frederick Manchester)
VEDIC RELIGION AND PHILOSOPHY

Translations

THE WISDOM OF GOD (Srimad Bhagavatam)
SHANKARA'S CREST-JEWEL OF DISCRIMI-
    NATION (with Christopher Isherwood)
THE SONG OF GOD: BHAGAVAD-GITA (with
    Isherwood)
HOW TO KNOW GOD, THE YOGA APHORISMS
    OF PATANJALI (with Isherwood)
SWAMI PREMANANDA: TEACHINGS AND
    REMINISCENCES

THE UPANISHADS

Breath of the Eternal

Translated by

SWAMI PRABHAVANANDA
FREDERICK MANCHESTER

VEDANTA PRESS
Hollywood, California

Hardback edition   ISBN 0-87481-037-X
Paperback edition   ISBN 0-87481-040-X

Library of Congress Catalog Card Number: 48-5935

PRINTED IN THE UNITED STATES OF AMERICA

If you wish to learn more about the teachings contained in this book, feel free to contact the Secretary, Vedanta Society of So. Calif., 1946 Vedanta Pl., Hollywood CA 90068 USA. You can also e-mail us at info@vedanta.org.

Visit our two web sites:
www.vedanta.org for information on Vedanta.
www.vedanta.com our online book catalog. (Phone: 800-816-2242)

PREFACE

It HAS SEEMED to me fitting that this translation of the Upanishads should be accompanied by a word regarding its principal author, Swami Prabhavananda.

The first intimation that the future Swami was to take up the religious life came when at the age of thirteen he read *The Gospel of Sri Ramakrishna* —a capacious volume in which a disciple of the great nineteenth-century saint told in faithful detail of the Master's day-by-day life and conversation. It was prophetic that the boy was vividly impressed by what he read there of Swami Brahmananda, partly because of something that attracted him even in the Swami's monastic name, and partly because of the acknowledged position of Swami Brahmananda as in a special sense the spiritual son of the saint.

Shortly after this first reading of the Gospel, Swami Prabhavananda met a disciple of Sri Ramakrishna, and also Sri Ramakrishna's widow, known to devotees as Holy Mother. A few years later, when he was eighteen, he met for the first time Swami Brahmananda himself. "I was imme-

diately drawn to him," says Swami Prabhavananda, "as if to a long-lost friend who was very
near and dear to me. I had never felt such a love
before in my life; it was the love of parents and
the love of a friend, all in one." Within three
months of this meeting the call to religion came in
urgent form, and the youth responded with the
resolution to be expected of the Kshatriya that he
was. One thing only mattered to him—that he
should go at once to Swami Brahmananda, who at
the time was living in a monastery at the foot of
the Himalayas, in the extreme north of India. He
had been told that the holy man did not welcome
unannounced visitors—but what of that! With
money originally intended for college fees and ex-
penses he made his long way from Calcutta to the
mountains. It was four o'clock of a morning, and
still dark, when he entered the monastery grounds
and found himself in the midst of many bunga-
lows, in one of which—but which one?—he
might expect to find the object of his journey. He
walked straight to a veranda to wait beside a door,
but before he could sit down Swami Brahmananda
himself came out by this same door, and his secretary by another. Seeing the boy, Swami Brahmananda said simply: "Hello! You are here," and
turning to his secretary, "Make room for him. He
will be staying."

Swami Prabhavananda was initiated as Swami
Brahmananda's disciple. He wanted to join the
monastery at once, but was not permitted to do
so. At the end of a month his spiritual master sent
him back to college to finish his education.

There followed a period of two years during
which religious interests gave way in his mind to
political. For the first time in Bengal, a revolution
was brewing against British rule, and with pa-
triotic ardor, and characteristic courage, Swami
Prabhavananda gave such assistance as his youth
and apparent guilelessness best fitted him to give.
It seemed to him then that the great duty of the
Hindu was to fight for freedom, and therefore that
to retire from the world into the monastic life was,
for him at least, indefensible. At twenty he grad-
uated from the City College of Calcutta and immediately entered upon a half-year of further study
in the department of philosophy of Calcutta Uni-
versity College.

It was during a brief vacation that his fate was
finally settled. In order to study Shankara with
Swami Shuddhananda, a Sanskrit scholar of great
repute, and a disciple of the world-famous Swami
Vivekananda, he went to live at Belur Math, the
great monastery on the Ganges near Calcutta.
Here, daily, Swami Shuddhananda would argue
with him on the subject of the monastic life and

urge him to become a monk. Swami Prabhavananda's vigorous opposition continued—but not
for long, for another and a compelling influence
was at work. Swami Brahmananda was staying in
the monastery at the time, and Swami Prabhavananda was much with him.

"One morning," says the Swami, telling of the
decisive moment, "when I went as usual to prostrate myself before Maharaj"—as Swami Brahmananda was called—"a bystander asked: 'When is
this boy going to become a monk?' Maharaj
looked me up and down, and quietly answered,
'When the Lord wills.' And as he said these words,
and as he looked at me, in his eyes an unforgettable
sweetness, all my revolutionary ideas were sud-
denly revolutionized, and I went downstairs and
said to Swami Shuddhananda: 'I have joined the
monastery.' "

Speaking of Swami Brahmananda, still a young
man, Sri Ramakrishna once said: "Rakhal has the
keen intelligence of a king. If he chose, he could
rule a large kingdom." This remark had an ap-
propriate sequel. During the last twenty years of
Swami Brahmananda's life, he served, with great
success, as head of the Ramakrishna Order. His
executive talents were matched by his spiritual distinction. On the occasion of Swami Prabhavananda's departure from India, when he was chosen

by his superiors as a representative of the Hindu
religion in America, a disciple of Sri Ramakrishna
said to him, referring to Swami Brahmananda,
"Never forget that you have seen a Son of God.
You have seen God."

This, then, was the man of whom Swami Prabhavananda was a disciple, and under whose guid-
ance he passed a dozen years of his life. During
four or five months of this period master and disciple lived in the closest intimacy; and to hear the
Swami speak of this experience is to realize that
into the fashioning of a monk, as this process was
conceived by Swami Brahmananda, there entered
the bitter as well as the sweet—the bitter itself,
however, being only the last and surest proof of
the sweetness. Whom the Lord loveth he chas-
teneth. On one occasion Swami Prabhavananda
was so cast down by the rebukes of his master that
he decided to desert the monastery and hide himself forever. With this thought in mind, he went
to prostrate himself before Maharaj and silently
take leave of him. Maharaj told him to sit down,
and for a while continued his earnest admonitions,
reminding his disciple of all his faults; then with
a sudden change of manner he asked: "Do you
think you can run away from me?" The kind
words the master then spoke dispelled all the
young man's sorrow. "Never before," Swami

Prabhavananda says, "had I been so deeply aware of his love and protection. All thought of running away was forgotten. His words soothed my burning heart. Then he said: 'Our love is so deep that we do not let you know how much we love you.'"

The sum of what I have been trying to say is this: that Swami Prabhavananda brings to his interpretation of the Upanishads not only a scholarly acquaintance with the Sanskrit texts, but also the insight to be derived from close association with one who embodied in his own mind and spirit, in the highest degree, the great intellectual and spiritual tradition of India. He has been the disciple of the disciple of one who has come to be regarded in India as the latest in its list of authentic avatars.

Our aim in this translation has not been to achieve a literal rendering but rather, allowing ourselves such freedom as seemed desirable, to convey in clear and simple English the sense and spirit of the original. Often for example, when we had a choice between following the text exactly and then explaining it in a note, or else expanding the text to include the necessary explanations, we have adopted the second alternative. In the opening of certain Upanishads, where a literal rendering would have resulted in an unattractive abruptness or baldness, we have—we trust discreetly—supplied a few

words. And, generally, we have felt free to resort
to paraphrase, to vary the order of detail, sometimes to omit words or phrases, perhaps even now
and again a sentence, so long as we faithfully preserved the substance and intent. In short, we have
designed this translation rather for the general pub-
lic, coming to the Upanishads for spiritual food,
than for the professional Sanskrit scholar.

With minor exception the original texts here
rendered are in verse. With minor exception, we
have employed prose. Despite what might have
been a natural temptation, we have made no effort
to use the language of the King James Version of
the Bible, but rather the contrary, feeling that by
abstaining in this regard we should better preserve
for the Hindu scripture its special character.

The Sanskrit Atman, meaning the God within,
we have everywhere translated by Self, though the
verbal equivalent of this expression appears nowhere in Hindu philosophy. We have thought it
better to benefit from the association with which
usage has already enriched the English word, than
to attempt to naturalize a foreign expression alto-
gether devoid, for Western readers, of spiritual
connotation. The syllable OM—symbol of Brahman, or God—is, to the Hindu, divine; and in
their rituals it is uttered with a solemn resonance,

indefinitely prolonged. Our typographical form for
the recurrent salutation or benediction:

> OM . . . Peace—peace—peace.

is designed to suggest as nearly as possible the mode
in which it is intoned.

The departures from prose are slight. In the
chants which precede the several Upanishads, and
especially in the hymn with which the Swetasvatara concludes, we use a form which is not prose,
nor perhaps verse either, save by courtesy, but
which has seemed to us to produce a heightened
effect not readily obtainable in ordinary prose. For
the hymn, a heightened effect seems particularly desirable, since in it both substance and form achieve
a poetic quality which the Upanishads do not elsewhere equal. Indeed, the form we have used was
the result of accident rather than design. Such a
passage as

> *Thou art the fire,*
> *Thou art the sun,*
> *Thou art the air,*
> *Thou art the moon,*
> *Thou art the starry firmament,*
> *Thou art Brahman Supreme:*
> *Thou art the waters—thou,*
> *The creator of all!*

—such a passage set down in the sober ways of prose seemed cribbed, confined—it asked for wings, however weak; and once we had yielded to the solicitation of capital letters and short rhythmic lines for matter such as this, we thought it well to complete the hymn as best we could in the same style.

The apparent arguments subjoined to the titles on the interleaves are not really arguments, since they give no proportioned epitome of the parts they precede. Rather they indicate dominant themes.

It remains to say a word regarding my part in the book. It is secondary. As one native to English speech, I have done what I could to help Swami Prabhavananda in his undertaking. He alone assumes responsibility for all ideas and opinions, all interpretations, and all statements of fact.

FREDERICK MANCHESTER

CONTENTS

INTRODUCTION

THE OLDEST SCRIPTURES of India, and the most important, are the Vedas. All orthodox Hindus recognize in them the origin of their faith and its highest written authority.

The Vedas are four in number: Rik, Sama, Yajur, and Atharva. Each of these is divided into two parts: Work and Knowledge. The first is mainly made up of hymns, instructions regarding rites and ceremonies, and rules of conduct. The second is concerned with knowledge of God, the highest aspect of religious truth, and is called—Upanishads.

The literal meaning of *upanishad*, "sitting near devotedly," brings picturesquely to mind an earnest disciple learning from his teacher. The word also means "secret teaching"—secret, no doubt, because a teaching vouchsafed only to those who are spiritually ready to receive and profit by it. Still another interpretation is sponsored by the great seventh-century commentator Shankara: knowledge of God—"the knowledge of Brahman, the knowledge that destroys the bonds of ignorance and leads to the supreme goal of freedom."

How many Upanishads once existed is unknown. One hundred and eight have been preserved, these ranging in length from a few hundred to many thousands of words, some in prose, some in verse, some part one, part the other. In style and manner they vary widely, often within the same Upanishad, being now simply and concretely narrative, now subtly and abstractly expository, often assuming, in either case, a dialogue form. Their tone too fluctuates, the characteristic seriousness and elevation finding occasional relief in homely humor. Who wrote them no one knows, nor, with any accuracy, when they were written. The Rishis whose insight they embody remain wholly in the background, impersonal as the truth they stood for, their individual lives lost forever, and even their names—

In the dark backward and abysm of time.

Of the one hundred and eight extant Upanishads, sixteen were recognized by Shankara as authentic and authoritative. On ten of these he wrote elaborate commentaries, which included quotations from the other six; and it is these ten which have come to be regarded as the principal Upanishads. Following are their names: Isha, Kena, Katha, Prasna, Mundaka, Mandukya, Taittiriya, Aitareya, Chandogya, Brihadaranyaka. Together they constitute, and will probably always constitute, the primary object of attention for all who would know the Hindu religion.

A characteristic of the Upanishads is their homogeneity. Many apparently differing conceptions are to be found in them, but these are, roughly speaking, to be found in all of them, not distributed, one in one Upanishad, another in another. It is true that one Upanishad may emphasize certain ideas, or a certain view, more than the rest, or may specialize as it were in a particular topic; but such distinctions often seem purely accidental, and are never important. The partitions between the Upanishads might therefore, for all practical purposes, be completely done away with, the whole hundred and eight being reduced to one.

Another and more important characteristic arises from the fact that the Upanishads are the work of saints and seers. Their authors were concerned with reporting insights which came to them in thought or vision, not with making these insights superficially coherent. They were not builders of systems but recorders of experience. We must be prepared, therefore, for apparent inconsistency, for obliviousness to one conception through temporary absorption in another. Nowhere must we expect to find the whole truth gathered together once for all in easy, triumphant, conscious formulation.

Still another characteristic of the Upanishads has to do with their form. Never were ideas set down —an expositor might suspect—with less regard for his convenience. Nowhere is there a logical beginning, nowhere a logical end. Furthermore, attention at all points is not upon parts, clearly recognized as parts, but upon wholes—upon brief, comprehensive, unanalyzed statement, it may be, or upon such particular elements as round out, when taken together, a momentary conception.

For the study of the Vedas, according to long tradition, and even according to the Vedas themselves, one must have a master, or Guru: "Approach a teacher," we read in the Rik, "with humility and with a desire to serve"; and in the Upanishads: "To many it is not given to hear of THAT"—meaning God—"which dwells in eternity. Many, though they hear of it, do not understand it. Wonderful is he who speaks of it. Intelligent is he who learns of it. Blessed is he who, taught by a good teacher, is able to comprehend it."

The function of the good teacher, as Hinduism conceives him, is twofold. He of course explains the scriptures, the spirit as well as the letter; but, what is more important still, he teaches by his life—by his daily acts, by his most casual words, sometimes even by his silence. Only to be near him, only to serve and obey him in humility and in reverence, is to become quickened in spirit; and the purpose of study of the scriptures is not merely or primarily to inform the intellect, but to purify and enrich the soul:

Pleasant indeed are the study and the teaching of the Vedas!
He who engages in these things attains to concentration
And is no longer a slave to his passions;
Devout, self-controlled, disciplined in spirit,
He rises to fame and is a blessing to mankind.

We have said that the orthodox Hindu regards the Vedas as his highest written authority. Any subsequent scripture, if he is to regard it as valid, must be in agreement with them: it may expand upon them, it may develop them, and still be recognized, but it must not contradict them. They are to him, as nearly as any human document can be, the expression of divine truth. At the same time it would be a mistake to suppose that his allegiance to their authority is slavish or blind. If he considers them the word of God, it is because he believes their truth to be verifiable, immediately, at any moment, in his own personal experience. If he found on due examination that it was not so verifiable, he would reject it. If he found that any

part of it was not so verifiable, he would reject
that. And in this position the scriptures, he will
tell you, uphold him. The real study, say the
Upanishads, is not study of themselves but study
of that "by which we realize the changeless." In
other words, the real study in religion is first-
hand experience of God.

Indeed the term Vedas, as used by the orthodox,
not only names a large body of texts handed down
by generation after generation, but in another
sense stands for nothing less than the inexpressible
truth of which all scriptures are of necessity a pale
reflection. Regarded in this second aspect, the
Vedas are infinite and eternal. They are that perfect knowledge which is God. They are identical,
in short, with the Word of the Christian St. John:
"In the beginning was the Word, and the Word
was with God, and the Word was God."

THE UPANISHADS

Breath of the Eternal

As smoke and sparks arise from a lighted fire kindled with damp fuel, even so, Maitreyi, have breathed forth from the Eternal all knowledge and all wisdom—what we know as the Rig Veda, the Yajur Veda, and the rest. They are the breath of the Eternal.

—BRIHADARANYAKA

I

ISHA

LIFE in the world and life in the spirit
are not incompatible. Work, or action,
is not contrary to knowledge of God,
but indeed, if performed without attachment, is a means to it. On the other
hand, renunciation is renunciation of
the ego, of selfishness—not of life. The
end, both of work and of renunciation,
is to know the Self within and Brahman without, and to realize their identity. The Self is Brahman, and Brahman is all.

ISHA

Filled   with Brahman are the things we see,
Filled   with Brahman are the things we see not,
From out of Brahman floweth all that is:
From Brahman all—yet is he still the same.
OM . . . Peace—peace—peace.

IN THE HEART of all things, of whatever there is in the universe, dwells the Lord. He alone is the reality. Wherefore, renouncing vain appearances, rejoice in him. Covet no man's wealth.

Well may he be content to live a hundred years who acts without attachment—who works his work with earnestness, but without desire, not yearning for its fruits—he, and he alone.

Worlds there are without suns, covered up with darkness. To these after death go the ignorant, slayers of the Self.

The Self is one. Unmoving, it moves swifter than thought. The senses do not overtake it, for always it goes before. Remaining still, it outstrips all that run. Without the Self, there is no life.

To the ignorant the Self appears to move—yet

3

it moves not. From the ignorant it is far distant—
yet it is near. It is within all, and it is without all.

He who sees all beings in the Self, and the Self
in all beings, hates none.

To the illumined soul, the Self is all. For him
who sees everywhere oneness, how can there be
delusion or grief?

The Self is everywhere. Bright is he, bodiless,
without scar of imperfection, without bone, without flesh, pure, untouched by evil. The Seer, the
Thinker, the One who is above all, the Self-
Existent—he it is that has established perfect
order among objects and beings from beginningless time.

To darkness are they doomed who devote themselves only to life in the world, and to a greater
darkness they who devote themselves only to
meditation.

Life in the world alone leads to one result,
meditation alone leads to another. So have we
heard from the wise.

They who devote themselves both to life in the
world and to meditation, by life in the world
overcome death, and by meditation achieve immortality.

To darkness are they doomed who worship
only the body, and to greater darkness they who
worship only the spirit.

Worship of the body alone leads to one result, worship of the spirit leads to another. So have we heard from the wise.

They who worship both the body and the spirit, by the body overcome death, and by the spirit achieve immortality.[1]

The face of truth is hidden by thy golden orb, O Sun. That do thou remove, in order that I who am devoted to truth may behold its glory.[2]

O nourisher, only seer, controller of all—O illumining Sun, fountain of life for all creatures—withhold thy light, gather together thy rays. May I behold through thy grace thy most blessed form. The Being that dwells therein—even that Being am I.

Let my life now merge in the all-pervading life. Ashes are my body's end. OM . . . O mind, remember Brahman. O mind, remember thy past deeds. Remember Brahman. Remember thy past deeds.

O god Agni, lead us to felicity. Thou knowest all our deeds. Preserve us from the deceitful attrac-

[1] In the Sanskrit this verse and the five preceding are exceedingly obscure. Commentators explain them variously, and not very clearly.

[2] In this verse, the Sun symbolizes the Self or Brahman, as is usual in the Vedas. The golden orb, like the rays and the light of the following verse, is Maya, the world of appearance.

tion of sin. To thee we offer our salutations, again
and yet again!¹

¹ This verse and the preceding constitute a prayer uttered
at the moment of death. Even today they are employed
by the Hindus in their funeral rites. The mind is exhorted
to   remember its past deeds because it is these deeds that
accompany the departing soul and determine the nature of
its next incarnation. Since cremation involves fire, it is
natural that it should be presided over by the god of fire,
Agni. The god is here invoked both in his own character
and as a symbol of Brahman.

II

KENA

THE power behind every activity of nature and of man is the power of Brahman. To realize this truth is to be immortal.

KENA

May quietness descend upon my limbs,
My speech, my breath, my eyes, my ears;
May all my senses wax clear and strong.
May Brahman show himself unto me.
Never may I deny Brahman, nor Brahman me.
I with him and he with me—may we abide always
    together.
May there be revealed to me,
Who am devoted to Brahman,
The holy truth of the Upanishads.
OM . . . Peace—peace—peace.

AT WHOSE BEHEST does the mind think? Who
bids the body live? Who makes the tongue speak?
Who is that effulgent Being that directs the eye
to form and color and the ear to sound?

The Self is ear of the ear, mind of the mind,
speech of the speech. He is also breath of the
breath, and eye of the eye. Having given up the
false identification of the Self with the senses and
the mind, and knowing the Self to be Brahman,
the wise, on departing this world, become immortal.

Him the eye does not see, nor the tongue ex-

9

press, nor the mind grasp. Him we neither know nor are able to teach. Different is he from the known, and different is he from the unknown. So have we heard from the wise.

That which cannot be expressed in words but by which the tongue speaks—know that to be Brahman. Brahman is not the being who is worshiped of men.

That which is not comprehended by the mind but by which the mind comprehends—know that to be Brahman. Brahman is not the being who is worshiped of men.

That which is not seen by the eye but by which the eye sees—know that to be Brahman. Brahman is not the being who is worshiped of men.

That which is not heard by the ear but by which the ear hears—know that to be Brahman. Brahman is not the being who is worshiped of men.

That which is not drawn by the breath but by which the breath is drawn—know that to be Brahman. Brahman is not the being who is worshiped of men.

If you think that you know well the truth of Brahman, know that you know little. What you think to be Brahman in your self, or what you think to be Brahman in the gods—that is not

Brahman. What is indeed the truth of Brahman you must therefore learn.

I cannot say that I know Brahman fully. Nor can I say that I know him not. He among us knows him best who understands the spirit of the words: "Nor do I know that I know him not."

He truly knows Brahman who knows him as beyond knowledge; he who thinks that he knows, knows not. The ignorant think that Brahman is known, but the wise know him to be beyond knowledge.

He who realizes the existence of Brahman behind every activity of his being—whether sensation, perception, or thought—he alone gains immortality. Through knowledge of Brahman comes power. Through knowledge of Brahman comes victory over death.

Blessed is the man who while he yet lives realizes Brahman. The man who realizes him not suffers his greatest loss. When they depart this life, the wise, who have realized Brahman as the Self in all beings, become immortal.

Once the gods won a victory over the demons, and though they had done so only through the power of Brahman, they were exceedingly vain. They thought to themselves, "It was we who beat our enemies, and the glory is ours."

Brahman saw their vanity and appeared before them. But they did not recognize him.

Then the other gods said to the god of fire: "Fire, find out for us who this mysterious spirit is."

"Yes," said the god of fire, and approached the spirit. The spirit said to him:

"Who are you?"

"I am the god of fire. As a matter of fact, I am very widely known."

"And what power do you wield?"

"I can burn anything on earth."

"Burn this," said the spirit, placing a straw before him.

The god of fire fell upon it with all his might, but could not consume it. So he ran back to the other gods, and said:

"I cannot discover who this mysterious spirit is."

Then said the other gods to the god of wind: "Wind, do you find out for us who he is."

"Yes," said the god of wind, and approached the spirit. The spirit said to him:

"Who are you?"

"I am the god of wind. As a matter of fact, I am very widely known. I fly swiftly through the heavens."

"And what power do you wield?"

"I can blow away anything on earth."

"Blow this away," said the spirit, placing a straw before him.

The god of wind fell upon it with all his might, but was unable to move it. So he ran back to the other gods, and said:

"I cannot discover who this mysterious spirit is."

Then said the other gods to Indra, greatest of them all: "O respected one, find out for us, we pray you, who he is."

"Yes," said Indra, and drew nigh to the spirit. But the spirit vanished, and in his place stood Uma, God the Mother, well adorned and of exceeding beauty. Beholding her, Indra asked:

"Who was the spirit that appeared to us?"

"That," answered Uma, "was Brahman. Through him it was, not of yourselves, that you attained your victory and your glory."

Thus did Indra, and the god of fire, and the god of wind, come to recognize Brahman.

The god of fire, the god of wind, and Indra—these excelled other gods, for they approached nearest to Brahman, and were the first to recognize him.

But of all gods Indra is supreme, for he approached nearest of the three to Brahman, and was the first of the three to recognize him.

This is the truth of Brahman in relation to nature: whether in the flash of the lightning, or in the wink of the eyes, the power that is shown is the power of Brahman.

This is the truth of Brahman in relation to man: in the motions of the mind, the power that is shown is the power of Brahman. For this reason should a man meditate upon Brahman by day and by night.

Brahman is the adorable being in all beings. Meditate upon him as such. He who meditates upon him as such is honored by all other beings.

A Disciple

Sir, teach me more of the knowledge of Brahman.

The Master

I have told you the secret knowledge. Austerity, self-control, performance of duty without attachment—these are the body of that knowledge. The Vedas are its limbs. Truth is its very soul.

He who attains to knowledge of Brahman, being freed from all evil, finds the Eternal, the Supreme.

OM . . . Peace—peace—peace.

III

KATHA

THE secret of immortality is to be found in purification of the heart, in meditation, in realization of the identity of the Self within and Brahman without. For immortality is simply union with God.

KATHA

Om . . .
May Brahman protect us,
May he guide us,
May he give us strength and right understanding.
May love and harmony be with us all.
OM . . . Peace—peace—peace.

ON A CERTAIN OCCASION Vajasrabasa, hoping for divine favor, performed a rite which required that he should give away all his possessions. He was careful, however, to sacrifice only his cattle, and of these only such as were useless— the old, the barren, the blind, and the lame. Observing this niggardliness, Nachiketa, his young son, whose heart had received the truth taught in the scriptures, thought to himself: "Surely a worshiper who dares bring such worthless gifts is doomed to utter darkness!" Thus reflecting, he came to his father, and cried:

"Father, I too belong to thee: to whom givest thou *me?*"

His father did not answer; but when Nachiketa asked the question again and yet again, he replied impatiently:

"Thee I give to Death!"

Then Nachiketa thought to himself: "Of my father's many sons and disciples I am indeed the best, or at least of the middle rank, not the worst; but of what good am I to the King of Death?" Yet being determined to keep his father's word he said:

"Father, do not repent thy vow! Consider how it has been with those that have gone before, and how it will be with those that now live. Like corn, a man ripens and falls to the ground; like corn, he springs up again in his season."

Having thus spoken, the boy journeyed to the house of Death.

But the god was not at home, and for three nights Nachiketa waited. When at length the King of Death returned, he was met by his servants, who said to him:

"A Brahmin, like to a flame of fire, entered thy house as guest, and thou wast not there. Therefore must a peace offering be made to him. With all accustomed rites, O King, thou must receive thy guest, for if a householder show not due hospitality to a Brahmin, he will lose what he most desires—the merits of his good deeds, his righteousness, his sons, and his cattle."

Then the King of Death approached Nachiketa and welcomed him with courteous words.

"O Brahmin," he said, "I salute thee. Thou
art indeed a guest worthy of all reverence. Let, I
pray thee, no harm befall me! Three nights hast
thou passed in my house and hast not received my
hospitality; ask of me, therefore, three boons—one
for each night."

"O Death," replied Nachiketa, "so let it be. And
as the first of these boons I ask that my father be
not anxious about me, that his anger be appeased,
and that when thou sendest me back to him, he
recognize me and welcome me."

"By my will," declared Death, "thy father shall
recognize thee and love thee as heretofore; and seeing thee again alive, he shall be tranquil of mind,
and he shall sleep in peace."

Then said Nachiketa: "In heaven there is no
fear at all. Thou, O Death, art not there, nor in
that place does the thought of growing old make
one tremble. There, free from hunger and from
thirst, and far from the reach of sorrow, all rejoice
and are glad. Thou knowest, O King, the fire
sacrifice that leads to heaven. Teach me that sacrifice, for I am full of faith. This is my second
wish."

Whereupon, consenting, Death taught the boy
the fire sacrifice, and all the rites and ceremonies
attending it. Nachiketa repeated all that he had
learned, and Death, well pleased with him, said:

"I grant thee an extra boon. Henceforth shall this sacrifice be called the Nachiketa Sacrifice, after thy name. Choose now thy third boon."

And then Nachiketa considered within himself, and said:

"When a man dies, there is this doubt: Some say, he is; others say, he is not. Taught by thee, I would know the truth. This is my third wish."

"Nay," replied Death, "even the gods were once puzzled by this mystery. Subtle indeed is the truth regarding it, not easy to understand. Choose thou some other boon, O Nachiketa."

But Nachiketa would not be denied.

"Thou sayest, O Death, that even the gods were once puzzled by this mystery, and that it is not easy to understand. Surely there is no teacher better able to explain it than thou—and there is no other boon equal to this."

To which, trying Nachiketa again, the god replied:

"Ask for sons and grandsons who shall live a hundred years. Ask for cattle, elephants, horses, gold. Choose for thyself a mighty kingdom. Or if thou canst imagine aught better, ask for that—not for sweet pleasures only but for the power, beyond all thought, to taste their sweetness. Yea, verily, the supreme enjoyer will I make thee of every good thing. Celestial maidens, beautiful to behold, such indeed as were not meant for mortals—even these, together with their bright chariots and their musical instruments, will I give unto thee, to serve thee. But for the secret of death, O Nachiketa, do not ask!"

But Nachiketa stood fast, and said: "These things endure only till the morrow, O Destroyer of Life, and the pleasures they give wear out the senses. Keep thou therefore horses and chariots, keep dance and song, for thyself! How shall he desire wealth, O Death, who once has seen thy face? Nay, only the boon that I have chosen— that only do I ask. Having found out the society of the imperishable and the immortal, as in knowing thee I have done, how shall I, subject to decay and death, and knowing well the vanity of the flesh—how shall I wish for long life?

"Tell me, O King, the supreme secret regarding which men doubt. No other boon will I ask."

Whereupon the King of Death, well pleased at heart, began to teach Nachiketa the secret of immortality.

King of Death

The good is one thing; the pleasant is another. These two, differing in their ends, both prompt to action. Blessed are they that choose the good; they that choose the pleasant miss the goal.

Both the good and the pleasant present themselves to men. The wise, having examined both,
distinguish the one from the other. The wise
prefer the good to the pleasant; the foolish, driven
by fleshly desires, prefer the pleasant to the good.

Thou, O Nachiketa, having looked upon fleshly
desires, delightful to the senses, hast renounced
them all. Thou hast turned from the miry way
wherein many a man wallows.

Far from each other, and leading to different
ends, are ignorance and knowledge. Thee, O
Nachiketa, I regard as one who aspires after
knowledge, for a multitude of pleasant objects
were unable to tempt thee.

Living in the abyss of ignorance yet wise in
their own conceit, deluded fools go round and
round, the blind led by the blind.

To the thoughtless youth, deceived by the
vanity of earthly possessions, the path that leads to
the eternal abode is not revealed. *This world alone
is real; there is no hereafter*—thinking thus, he
falls again and again, birth after birth, into my
jaws.

To many it is not given to hear of the Self.
Many, though they hear of it, do not understand
it. Wonderful is he who speaks of it. Intelligent is
he who learns of it. Blessed is he who, taught by
a good teacher, is able to understand it.

The truth of the Self cannot be fully understood when taught by an ignorant man, for opinions regarding it, not founded in knowledge, vary one from another. Subtler than the subtlest is this Self, and beyond all logic. Taught by a teacher who knows the Self and Brahman as one, a man leaves vain theory behind and attains to truth.

The awakening which thou hast known does not come through the intellect, but rather, in fullest measure, from the lips of the wise. Beloved Nachiketa, blessed, blessed art thou, because thou seekest the Eternal. Would that I had more pupils like thee!

Well I know that earthly treasure lasts but till the morrow. For did not I myself, wishing to be King of Death, make sacrifice with fire? But the sacrifice was a fleeting thing, performed with fleeting objects, and small is my reward, seeing that only for a moment will my reign endure.

The goal of worldly desire, the glittering objects for which all men long, the celestial pleasures they hope to gain by religious rites, the most sought after of miraculous powers—all these were within thy grasp. But all these, with firm resolve, thou hast renounced.

The ancient, effulgent being, the indwelling Spirit, subtle, deep-hidden in the lotus of the heart, is hard to know. But the wise man, following the path of meditation, knows him, and is freed alike from pleasure and from pain.

The man who has learned that the Self is separate from the body, the senses, and the mind, and has fully known him, the soul of truth, the subtle principle—such a man verily attains to him, and is exceeding glad, because he has found the source and dwelling place of all felicity. Truly do I believe, O Nachiketa, that for thee the gates of joy stand open.

Nachiketa

Teach me, O King, I beseech thee, whatsoever thou knowest to be beyond right and wrong, beyond cause and effect, beyond past, present, and future.

King of Death

Of that goal which all the Vedas declare, which is implicit in all penances, and in pursuit of which men lead lives of continence and service, of that will I briefly speak.

It is—OM.

This syllable is Brahman. This syllable is indeed supreme. He who knows it obtains his desire.

It is the strongest support. It is the highest symbol. He who knows it is reverenced as a knower of Brahman.

The Self, whose symbol is OM, is the omniscient Lord. He is not born. He does not die. He is neither cause nor effect. This Ancient One is unborn, eternal, imperishable; though the body be destroyed, he is not killed.

If the slayer think that he slays, if the slain think that he is slain, neither of them knows the truth. The Self slays not, nor is he slain.

Smaller than the smallest, greater than the greatest, this Self forever dwells within the hearts of all. When a man is free from desire, his mind and senses purified, he beholds the glory of the Self and is without sorrow.

Though seated, he travels far; though at rest, he moves all things. Who but the purest of the pure can realize this Effulgent Being, who is joy and who is beyond joy.

Formless is he, though inhabiting form. In the midst of the fleeting he abides forever. All-pervading and supreme is the Self. The wise man, knowing him in his true nature, transcends all grief.

The Self is not known through study of the scriptures, nor through subtlety of the intellect, nor through much learning. But by him who longs for him is he known.[1] Verily unto him does the Self reveal his true being.

By learning a man cannot know him, if he desist not from evil, if he control not his senses, if he quiet not his mind, and practice not meditation.

To him Brahmins and Kshatriyas are but food, and death itself a condiment.

Both the individual self and the Universal Self have entered the cave of the heart, the abode of the Most High, but the knowers of Brahman and the householders who perform the fire sacrifices see a difference between them as between sunshine and shadow.

May we perform the Nachiketa Sacrifice, which bridges the world of suffering. May we know the imperishable Brahman, who is fearless, and who is the end and refuge of those who seek liberation.

Know that the Self is the rider, and the body the chariot; that the intellect is the charioteer, and the mind the reins.[2]

The senses, say the wise, are the horses; the roads they travel are the mazes of desire. The wise

---

[1] There is another interpretation of this sentence, involving the mystery of grace: "Whom the Self chooses, by him is he attained."

[2] In Hindu psychology the mind is the organ of perception.

call the Self the enjoyer when he is united with
the body, the senses, and the mind.

When a man lacks discrimination and his mind
is uncontrolled, his senses are unmanageable, like
the restive horses of a charioteer. But when a man
has discrimination and his mind is controlled, his
senses, like the well-broken horses of a charioteer,
lightly obey the rein.

He who lacks discrimination, whose mind is un-
steady and whose heart is impure, never reaches the
goal, but is born again and again. But he who has
discrimination, whose mind is steady and whose
heart is pure, reaches the goal, and having reached
it is born no more.

The man who has a sound understanding for
charioteer, a controlled mind for reins—he it is
that reaches the end of the journey, the supreme
abode of Vishnu, the all-pervading.[1]

The senses derive from physical objects, physical objects from mind, mind from intellect, intellect from ego, ego from the unmanifested seed, and
the unmanifested seed from Brahman—the Uncaused Cause.

Brahman is the end of the journey. Brahman is
the supreme goal.

This Brahman, this Self, deep-hidden in all

_____
[1] Vishnu is here equivalent to Brahman.

beings, is not revealed to all; but to the seers, pure in heart, concentrated in mind—to them is he revealed.

The senses of the wise man obey his mind, his mind obeys his intellect, his intellect obeys his ego, and his ego obeys the Self.

Arise! Awake! Approach the feet of the Master and know THAT. Like the sharp edge of a razor, the sages say, is the path. Narrow it is, and difficult to tread!

Soundless, formless, intangible, undying, tasteless, odorless, eternal, without beginning, without end, immutable, beyond nature, is the Self. Knowing him as such, one is freed from death.

The Narrator

The wise man, having heard and taught the eternal truth revealed by the King of Death to Nachiketa, is glorified in the heaven of Brahma.

He who sings with devotion this supreme secret in the assembly of the Brahmins, or at the rites in memory of his fathers, is rewarded with rewards immeasurable!

King of Death

The Self-Existent made the senses turn outward. Accordingly, man looks toward what is without, and sees not what is within. Rare is he who, longing for immortality, shuts his eyes to what is without and beholds the Self.

Fools follow the desires of the flesh and fall into the snare of all-encompassing death; but the wise, knowing the Self as eternal, seek not the things that pass away.

He through whom man sees, tastes, smells, hears, feels, and enjoys, is the omniscient Lord.

He, verily, is the immortal Self. Knowing him, one knows all things.

He through whom man experiences the sleeping or waking states is the all-pervading Self. Knowing him, one grieves no more.

He who knows that the individual soul, enjoyer of the fruits of action, is the Self—ever present within, lord of time, past and future—casts out all fear. For this Self is the immortal Self.

He who sees the First-Born—born of the mind of Brahma, born before the creation of waters—and sees him inhabiting the lotus of the heart, living among physical elements, sees Brahman indeed. For this First-Born is the immortal Self.[1]

That being who is the power of all powers, and

[1] Brahman, the absolute, impersonal existence, when associated with the power called Maya—the power to evolve as the empirical universe—is known as Hiranyagarbha, the First-Born.

is born as such, who embodies himself in the elements and in them exists, and who has entered the lotus of the heart, is the immortal Self.

Agni, the all-seeing, who lies hidden in fire sticks, like a child well guarded in the womb, who is worshiped day by day by awakened souls, and by those who offer oblations in sacrificial fire—he is the immortal Self.[1]

That in which the sun rises and in which it sets, that which is the source of all the powers of nature and of the senses, that which nothing can transcend—that is the immortal Self.

What is within us is also without. What is without is also within. He who sees difference between what is within and what is without goes evermore from death to death.

By the purified mind alone is the indivisible Brahman to be attained. Brahman alone is—nothing else is. He who sees the manifold universe, and not the one reality, goes evermore from death to death.

That being, of the size of a thumb, dwells deep

[1] The reference is to the Vedic sacrifice. Agni, whose name means fire, is said to be all-seeing, the fire symbolizing Brahman, the Revealer; the two fire sticks, which being rubbed together produce the fire, represent the heart and the mind of man.

within the heart.[1] He is the lord of time, past and future. Having attained him, one fears no more. He, verily, is the immortal Self.

That being, of the size of a thumb, is like a flame without smoke. He is the lord of time, past and future, the same today and tomorrow. He, verily, is the immortal Self.

As rain, fallen on a hill, streams down its side, so runs he after many births who sees manifoldness in the Self.

As pure water poured into pure water remains pure, so does the Self remain pure, O Nachiketa, uniting with Brahman.

To the Birthless, the light of whose consciousness forever shines, belongs the city of eleven gates.[2] He who meditates on the ruler of that city knows no more sorrow. He attains liberation, and for him there can no longer be birth or death. For the ruler of that city is the immortal Self.

The immortal Self is the sun shining in the sky, he is the breeze blowing in space, he is the fire burning on the altar, he is the guest dwelling in

[1] The sages ascribe a definite, minute size to the Self in order to assist the disciple in meditation.

[2] The Birthless is the Self; the city of eleven gates is the body with its apertures—eyes, ears, etc.

the house; he is in all men, he is in the gods, he is
in the ether, he is wherever there is truth; he is the
fish that is born in water, he is the plant that
grows in the soil, he is the river that gushes from
the mountain—he, the changeless reality, the
illimitable!

He, the adorable one, seated in the heart, is the
power that gives breath. Unto him all the senses
do homage.

What can remain when the dweller in this
body leaves the outgrown shell, since he is, verily,
the immortal Self?

Man does not live by breath alone, but by him
in whom is the power of breath.

And now, O Nachiketa, will I tell thee of the
unseen, the eternal Brahman, and of what befalls
the Self after death.

Of those ignorant of the Self, some enter into
beings possessed of wombs, others enter into
plants—according to their deeds and the growth
of their intelligence.

That which is awake in us even while we sleep,
shaping in dream the objects of our desire—that
indeed is pure, that is Brahman, and that verily is
called the Immortal. All the worlds have their
being in that, and none can transcend it. That is
the Self.

As fire, though one, takes the shape of every object which it consumes, so the Self, though one, takes the shape of every object in which it dwells.

As air, though one, takes the shape of every object which it enters, so the Self, though one, takes the shape of every object in which it dwells.

As the sun, revealer of all objects to the seer, is not harmed by the sinful eye, nor by the impurities of the objects it gazes on, so the one Self, dwelling in all, is not touched by the evils of the world. For he transcends all.

He is one, the lord and innermost Self of all; of one form, he makes of himself many forms. To him who sees the Self revealed in his own heart belongs eternal bliss—to none else, to none else!

Intelligence of the intelligent, eternal among the transient, he, though one, makes possible the desires of many. To him who sees the Self revealed in his own heart belongs eternal peace—to none else, to none else!

Nachiketa

How, O King, shall I find that blissful Self, supreme, ineffable, who is attained by the wise? Does he shine by himself, or does he reflect another's light?

King of Death

Him the sun does not illumine, nor the moon, nor the stars, nor the lightning—nor, verily, fires kindled upon earth. He is the one light that gives light to all. He shining, everything shines.

This universe is a tree eternally existing, its root aloft, its branches spread below. The pure root of the tree is Brahman, the immortal, in whom the three worlds have their being, whom none can transcend, who is verily the Self.[1]

The whole universe came forth from Brahman, moves in Brahman. Mighty and awful is he, like to a thunderbolt crashing loud through the heavens. For those who attain him death has no terror.

In fear of him fire burns, the sun shines, the rains fall, the winds blow, and death kills.

If a man fails to attain Brahman before he casts off his body, he must again put on a body in the world of created things.

In one's own soul Brahman is realized clearly, as if seen in a mirror. In the heaven of Brahma also is Brahman realized clearly, as one distinguishes light from darkness. In the world of the fathers he

[1] The "three worlds" are the sky, the earth, and the nether-world.

is beheld as in a dream.[1] In the world of angels
he appears as if reflected in water.

The senses have separate origin in their several
objects. They may be active, as in the waking
state, or they may be inactive, as in sleep. He who
knows them to be distinct from the changeless
Self grieves no more.

Above the senses is the mind. Above the mind
is the intellect. Above the intellect is the ego.
Above the ego is the unmanifested seed, the Primal
Cause.

And verily beyond the unmanifested seed is
Brahman, the all-pervading spirit, the unconditioned, knowing whom one attains to freedom and
achieves immortality.

None beholds him with the eyes, for he is without visible form. Yet in the heart is he revealed,
through self-control and meditation. Those who
know him become immortal.

When all the senses are stilled, when the mind
is at rest, when the intellect wavers not—that, say
the wise, is the highest state.

This calm of the senses and the mind has been
defined as yoga. He who attains it is freed from delusion.

[1] The fathers are the spirits of the meritorious dead who
dwell in another world, reaping the fruits of their good
deeds, but subject to rebirth.

In one not freed from delusion this calm is un-
certain, unreal: it comes and goes. Brahman words
cannot reveal, mind cannot reach, eyes cannot see.
How then, save through those who know him, can
he be known?

There are two selves, the apparent self and the
real Self. Of these it is the real Self, and he alone,
who must be felt as truly existing. To the man
who has felt him as truly existing he reveals his
innermost nature.

The mortal in whose heart desire is dead becomes immortal. The mortal in whose heart the
knots of ignorance are untied becomes immortal.
These are the highest truths taught in the scriptures.

Radiating from the lotus of the heart there are
a hundred and one nerves. One of these ascends
toward the thousand-petaled lotus in the brain.
If, when a man comes to die, his vital force passes
upward and out through this nerve, he attains immortality; but if his vital force passes out through
another nerve, he goes to one or another plane of
mortal existence, and remains subject to birth and
death.

The Supreme Person, of the size of a thumb,
the innermost Self, dwells forever in the hearts of
all beings. As one draws the pith from a reed, so
must the aspirant after truth, with great perse-

verance, separate the Self from the body. Know the Self to be pure and immortal—yea, pure and immortal!

The Narrator

Nachiketa, having learned from the god this knowledge and the whole process of yoga, was freed from impurities and from death, and was united with Brahman. Thus will it be with another also if he know the innermost Self.

OM . . . Peace—peace—peace.

IV

PRASNA

MAN is composed of such elements as vital breath, deeds, thought, and the senses—all of them deriving their being from the Self. They have come out of the Self, and in the Self they ultimately disappear—even as the waters of a river disappear in the sea.

PRASNA

OM . . .
With our ears may we hear what is good.
With our eyes may we behold thy righteousness.
Tranquil in body, may we who worship thee find rest.
OM . . . Peace—peace—peace.
OM . . . Hail to the supreme Self!

SUKESHA, Satyakama, Gargya, Kousalya, Bhargava, and Kabandhi, devotees and seekers after the truth of the supreme Brahman, with faith and humility approached the sage Pippalada.

Said the sage: Practice austerity, continence, faith for a year; then ask what questions you wish. If I can, I will answer.

After a year Kabandhi approached the teacher and asked:

"Sir, how did the creatures come into being?"

"The Lord of beings," replied the sage, "meditated and produced Prana, the primal energy, and Rayi, the giver of form, desiring that they, male and female, should in manifold ways produce creatures for him.

"Prana, the primal energy, is the sun; and Rayi, the form-giving substance, is the moon.

43

"Be it known that all this universe, that which is gross and that which is subtle, is one with Rayi. Therefore is Rayi omnipresent.

"In like manner is the universe one with Prana. The rising sun pervades the east, and fills with energy all beings that there inhabit; and likewise when his rays fall on the south, the west, the north, the zenith, the nadir, and the intermediate regions, to all beings that there inhabit he gives life.

"Prana is the soul of the universe, assuming all forms; he is the light that animates and illumines all: even as it is written—

"The wise know him who assumes all forms, who is radiant, who is all-knowing, who is the one light that gives light to all. He rises as the sun of a thousand rays, and abides in infinite places."

"Prana and Rayi, uniting, divide the year. Two are the paths of the sun—two are the paths that men travel after death. These are the southern and the northern.

"Those who desire offspring and are devoted to almsgiving and rituals, considering these the highest accomplishment, attain the world of the moon and are born again on earth. They travel by the southern path, which is the path of the fathers, and is indeed Rayi, the maker of forms.

"But those who are devoted to the worship of

the Self, by means of austerity, continence, faith,
and knowledge, go by the northern path and attain the world of the sun. The sun, the light, is
indeed the source of all energy. It is immortal, beyond fear; it is the supreme goal. For him who
goes to the sun there is no more birth nor death.
The sun ends birth and death.

"Prana and Rayi, uniting, form the month. Its
dark fortnight is Rayi, and its bright fortnight is
Prana. Sages perform their devotional rites in the
light, with knowledge; fools, in the dark, in ignorance.

"Food is Prana and Rayi. From food is produced seed, and from seed, in turn, are born all
creatures.

"Those who worship the world of creation produce children; but those alone attain the world of
Brahman who are steadfast in continence, meditation, and truthfulness.

"The pure world of Brahman is attainable by
those only who are neither deceitful, nor wicked,
nor false."

Then Bhargava approached the teacher and
asked:

"Holy sir, how many several powers hold together this body? Which of them are most manifest in it? And which is the greatest?"

"The powers," replied the sage, "are ether, air, fire, water, earth—these being the five elements which compose the body; and, besides these, speech, mind, eye, ear, and the rest of the sense organs. Once these powers made the boastful assertion: 'We hold the body together and support it,' whereupon Prana, the primal energy, supreme over them all, said to them: 'Do not deceive yourselves. It is I alone, dividing myself fivefold, who hold together this body and support it.' But they would not believe him.

"Prana, to justify himself, made as if he intended to leave the body. But as he rose and appeared to be going, all the rest realized that if he went they also would have to depart with him; and as Prana again seated himself, the rest found their respective places. As bees go out when their queen goes out, and return when she returns, so was it with speech, mind, vision, hearing, and the rest. Convinced of their error, the powers now praised Prana, saying:

" 'As fire, Prana burns; as the sun, he shines; as cloud, he rains; as Indra, he rules the gods; as wind, he blows; as the moon, he nourishes all. He is that which is visible and also that which is invisible. He is immortal life.

" 'As spokes in the nave of a wheel, so is everything made fast in Prana—the Rik, the Yajur,

the Sama, all sacrifices, the Kshatriyas, and the
Brahmins.

"'O Prana, lord of creation, thou movest in the
womb, and art born again. To thee who, as
breath, dwellest in the body, all creatures bring
offerings.

"'Thou, as fire, dost carry oblations to the
gods; and through thee the fathers receive their
offerings. To every organ of sense thou givest
its function.

"'Prana, thou art the creator; thou art the destroyer by thy prowess; and thou art the protector.
Thou movest in the sky as the sun, and lord of
lights art thou.

"'Prana, when thou showerest down rain, thy
creatures rejoice, hoping that they will find food,
as much as they desire.

"'Thou art purity itself, thou art the master
of all that exists, thou art fire, the eater of offerings. We, the organs of sense, offer to thee thy
food—to thee, the father of all.

"'That power of thine which dwells in speech,
in the ear, and in the eye, and which pervades the
heart—make that propitious, and forsake us not.

"'Whatsoever exists in the universe is depend-
ent on thee, O Prana. Protect us as a mother pro-
tects her children. Grant us prosperity and grant
us wisdom.'"

And when it was the turn of Kousalya, he put this question:

"Master, of what is Prana born; how does he enter the body; how does he live there after dividing himself; how does he go out; how does he experience what is outside; and how does he hold together the body, the senses, and the mind?"

To which the sage replied:

"Kousalya, you ask very difficult questions; but since you are a sincere seeker after the truth of Brahman, I must answer.

"Prana is born of the Self. Like a man and his shadow, the Self and Prana are inseparable. Prana enters the body at birth, that the desires of the mind, continuing from past lives, may be fulfilled.

"As a king employs officials to rule over different portions of his kingdom, so Prana associates with himself four other Pranas, each a portion of himself and each assigned a separate function.

"The *Prana* himself dwells in eye, ear, mouth, and nose; the *Apana*, which is the second Prana, rules the organs of excretion and generation; the *Samana*, which is the third Prana, inhabits the navel, and governs digestion and assimilation.

"The Self dwells in the lotus of the heart, whence radiate a hundred and one nerves. From each of these proceed one hundred others, which are smaller, and from each of these, again, seventy-two thousand others, which are smaller still. In all these moves the *Vyana*, which is the fourth Prana.

"And then at the moment of death, through the nerve in the center of the spine, the *Udana*, which is the fifth Prana, leads the virtuous man upward to higher birth, the sinful man downward to lower birth, and the man who is both virtuous and sinful to rebirth in the world of men.

"The sun is the Prana of the universe. It rises to help the Prana in the eye of man to see. The power of earth maintains the Apana in man. The ether between the sun and the earth is the Samana, and the all-pervading air is the Vyana. The Udana is fire, and therefore he whose bodily heat has gone out dies, after which his senses are absorbed in the mind, and he is born again.

"Whatever his thought at the moment of death, this it is that unites a man with Prana, who in turn, uniting himself with Udana and with the Self, leads the man to be reborn in the world he merits.

"The progeny of him who knows Prana as I have revealed him to you is never cut off; and he himself becomes immortal.

"It was said of old: *One who knows the Prana —whence he has his source, how he enters the body, how he lives there after dividing himself five-*

fold, *what are his inner workings—such an one attains to immortality, yea, even to immortality."*

Gargya then asked:

"Master, when a man's body sleeps, who is it within that sleeps, and who is awake, and who is dreaming? Who then experiences happiness, and with whom are all the sense organs united?"

"As the rays of the sun, O Gargya, when he sets," replied the sage, "gather themselves up in his disk of light, to come out again when he rises, so the senses gather themselves up in the mind, the highest of them all. Therefore when a man does not hear, see, smell, taste, touch, speak, grasp, enjoy, we say that he sleeps.

"Only the Pranas are then awake in the body, and the mind is led nearer to the Self.

"While in dream, the mind revives its past impressions. Whatever it has seen, it sees again; whatever it has heard, it hears again; whatever it has enjoyed in various countries and in various quarters of the earth, it enjoys again. What has been seen and not seen, heard and not heard, enjoyed and not enjoyed, both the real and the unreal, it sees; yea, it sees all.[1]

[1] Shankara, in explaining the above passage, remarks that by the unseen, the unheard, the unenjoyed that a man experiences in dreams are meant the things that were seen and heard and enjoyed in past lives.

"When the mind is overpowered by deep slumber, it dreams no more. It rests happily in the body.

"As birds, my friend, fly to the tree for rest, even so do all these things fly to the Self: earth and its peculiar essence, water and its peculiar essence, fire and its peculiar essence, air and its peculiar essence, ether and its peculiar essence, the eye and what it sees, the ear and what it hears, the nose and what it smells, the tongue and what it tastes, the skin and what it touches, the voice and what it speaks, the hands and what they grasp, the feet and what they walk on, the mind and what it perceives, the intellect and what it understands, the ego and what it appropriates, the heart and what it loves, light and what it illumines, energy and what it binds together.

"For verily it is the Self that sees, hears, smells, tastes, thinks, knows, acts. He is Brahman, whose essence is knowledge. He is the immutable Self, the Supreme.

"He who knows the immutable, the pure, the shadowless, the bodiless, the colorless, attains to Brahman, O my friend. Such an one becomes all-knowing, and he dwells in all beings. Of him it is written:

"He who knows that immutable Self, wherein live the mind, the senses, the Pranas, the elements

—*verily such an one knows all things, and realizes the Self in all.*"

Whereupon Satyakama, coming near to the master, said:

"Venerable sir, if a man meditate upon the syllable OM all his life, what shall be his reward after death?"

And the master answered him thus:

"Satyakama, OM is Brahman—both the conditioned and the unconditioned, the personal and the impersonal. By meditating upon it the wise man may attain either the one or the other.

"If he meditate upon OM with but little knowledge of its meaning, but nevertheless is enlightened thereby, upon his death he will be immediately born again on this earth, and during his new life he will be devoted to austerity, continence, and faith, and will attain to spiritual greatness.

"If, again, he meditate upon OM with a greater knowledge of its meaning, upon his death he will ascend to the lunar heaven, and after he has partaken of its pleasures will return again to earth.

"But if he meditate upon OM in the full consciousness that it is one with God, upon his death he will be united with the light that is in the sun, he will be freed from evil, even as a snake is freed from its slough, and he will ascend to God's dwelling place. There he will realize Brahman, who evermore abides in the heart of all beings— Brahman Supreme!

"Concerning the sacred syllable OM it is written:

"*The syllable OM, when it is not fully under- stood, does not lead beyond mortality. When it is fully understood, and meditation is therefore rightly directed, a man is freed from fear, whether he be awake, dreaming, or sleeping the dreamless sleep, and attains to Brahman.*

"By virtue of a little understanding of OM a man returns to earth after death. By virtue of a greater understanding he attains to the celestial sphere. By virtue of a complete understanding he learns what is known only to the seers. The sage, with the help of OM, reaches Brahman, the fear- less, the undecaying, the immortal!"

Lastly, Sukesa approached the sage and said:

"Holy sir, Hiranyanabha, prince of Kosala, once asked me this question, 'Sukesa, do you know the Self and his sixteen parts?' I replied, 'I do not. Surely, if I knew them, I would have taught them to you. I will not lie, for he who lies perishes, root and all.' The prince silently mounted his chariot and went away. So now I ask of thee, Where is the Self?"

The sage replied:

"My child, within this body dwells the Self, from whom sprang the sixteen parts of the universe; and in this manner they came into being:

"If, creating, I enter my creation," the Self reflected, "what is there to bind me to it; what is there to go out from it when I go out, to stay within it when I stay?" Pondering thus, and in answer to his thought, he made Prana; and from Prana he made desire; and from desire he made ether, air, fire, water, earth, the senses, the mind, and food; and from food he made vigor, penance, the Vedas, the sacrificial rites, and all the worlds. Thereafter, in the worlds, he created names. And the number of the elements he thus created was sixteen.

"As the flowing rivers, whose destination is the sea, having reached it disappear in it, losing their names and forms, and men speak only of the sea: so these sixteen parts created from out his own being by the Self, the Eternal Seer, having returned to him from whom they came, disappear in him, their destination, losing their names and forms, and people speak only of the Self. Then for man the sixteen parts are no more, and he attains to immortality.

"Thus was it said of old:

"*The sixteen parts are spokes projecting from the Self, who is the hub of the wheel. The Self*

*is the goal of knowledge. Know him and go be-
yond death."*

The sage concluded, saying:

"What I have told you is all that can be said
about the Self, the Supreme Brahman. Beyond this
there is naught."

The disciples worshiped the sage, and said:

"You are indeed our father. You have led us
beyond the sea of ignorance.

"We bow down to all the great seers!

"Obeisance to the great seers!"

OM . . . Peace—peace—peace.

V

MUNDAKA

SINCE the manifold objects of sense are merely emanations of Brahman, to know them in themselves is not enough. Since all the actions of men are but phases of the universal process of creation, action alone is not enough.

The sage must distinguish between knowledge and wisdom. Knowledge is of things, acts, and relations. But wisdom is of Brahman alone; and, beyond all things, acts, and relations, he abides forever. To become one with him is the only wisdom.

MUNDAKA

OM . . .
With our ears may we hear what is good.
With our eyes may we behold thy righteousness.
Tranquil in body, may we who worship thee find rest.
OM . . . Peace—peace—peace.

OUT OF THE infinite ocean of existence arose Brahma, first-born and foremost among the gods. From him sprang the universe, and he became its protector. The knowledge of Brahman, the foundation of all knowledge, he revealed to his first-born son, Atharva.

In turn Atharva taught this same knowledge of Brahman to Angi. Angi, again, taught it to Satyabaha, who revealed it to Angiras.

To Angiras came upon a time Sounaka, the famous householder, and asked respectfully:

"Holy sir, what is that by which all else is known?"

"Those who know Brahman," replied Angiras, "say that there are two kinds of knowledge, the higher and the lower.

"The lower is knowledge of the Vedas (the Rik, the Sama, the Yajur, and the Atharva), and

59

also of phonetics, ceremonials, grammar, etymol-
ogy, metre, and astronomy.

"The higher is knowledge of that by which one
knows the changeless reality. By this is fully revealed to the wise that which transcends the senses,
which is uncaused, which is indefinable, which has
neither eyes nor ears, neither hands nor feet, which
is all-pervading, subtler than the subtlest—the
everlasting, the source of all.

"As the web comes out of the spider and is
withdrawn, as plants grow from the soil and hair
from the body of man, so springs the universe
from the eternal Brahman.

"Brahman willed that it should be so, and
brought forth out of himself the material cause
of the universe; from this came the primal energy,
and from the primal energy mind, from mind the
subtle elements, from the subtle elements the many
worlds, and from the acts performed by beings
in the many worlds the chain of cause and effect—
the reward and punishment of works.

"Brahman sees all, knows all; he is knowledge
itself. Of him are born cosmic intelligence, name,
form, and the material cause of all created beings
and things."

Finite and transient are the fruits of sacrificial

rites. The deluded, who regard them as the highest good, remain subject to birth and death.

Living in the abyss of ignorance, yet wise in their own conceit, the deluded go round and round, like the blind led by the blind.

Living in the abyss of ignorance, the deluded think themselves blest. Attached to works, they know not God. Works lead them only to heaven, whence, to their sorrow, their rewards quickly exhausted, they are flung back to earth.

Considering religion to be observance of rituals and performance of acts of charity, the deluded remain ignorant of the highest good. Having enjoyed in heaven the reward of their good works, they enter again into the world of mortals.

But wise, self-controlled, and tranquil souls—who are contented in spirit, and who practice austerity and meditation in solitude and silence—are freed from all impurity, and attain by the path of liberation to the immortal, the truly existing, the changeless Self.

Let a man devoted to spiritual life examine carefully the ephemeral nature of such enjoyment, whether here or hereafter, as may be won by good works, and so realize that it is not by works that one gains the Eternal. Let him give no thought to transient things, but absorbed in meditation, let him renounce the world. To know the Eternal, let him humbly approach a Guru devoted to Brahman and well-versed in the scriptures.

To a disciple who approaches reverently, who is tranquil and self-controlled, the wise teacher gives that knowledge, faithfully and without stint, by which is known the truly existing, the changeless Self.

The Imperishable is the Real. As sparks innumerable fly upward from a blazing fire, so from the depths of the Imperishable arise all things. To the depths of the Imperishable they again descend.

Self-luminous is that Being, and formless. He dwells within all and without all. He is unborn, pure, greater than the greatest, without breath, without mind.

From him are born breath, mind, the organs of sense, ether, air, fire, water, and the earth, and he binds all these together.

Heaven is his head, the sun and moon his eyes, the four quarters his ears, the revealed scriptures his voice, the air his breath, the universe his heart. From his feet came the earth. He is the innermost Self of all.

From him arises the sun-illumined sky, from the sky the rain, from the rain food, and from food the seed in man which he gives to woman.

Thus do all creatures descend from him.

From him are born hymns, devotional chants, scriptures, rites, sacrifices, oblations, divisions of time, the doer and the deed, and all the worlds lighted by the sun and purified by the moon.

From him are born gods of diverse descent. From him are born angels, men, beasts, birds; from him vitality, and food to sustain it; from him austerity and meditation, faith, truth, continence, and law.

From him spring the organs of sense, their activities, and their objects, together with their awareness of these objects. All these things, parts of man's nature, spring from him.

In him the seas and the mountains have their source; from him spring the rivers, and from him the herbs and other life-sustaining elements, by the aid of which the subtle body of man subsists in the physical body.

Thus Brahman is all in all. He is action, knowledge, goodness supreme. To know him, hidden in the lotus of the heart, is to untie the knot of ignorance.

Self-luminous is Brahman, ever present in the hearts of all. He is the refuge of all, he is the supreme goal. In him exists all that moves and breathes. In him exists all that is. He is both that which is gross and that which is subtle. Adorable is he. Beyond the ken of the senses is he. Supreme is he. Attain thou him!

He, the self-luminous, subtler than the subtlest, in whom exist all the worlds and all those that live therein—he is the imperishable Brahman. He is the principle of life. He is speech, and he is mind. He is real. He is immortal. Attain him, O my friend, the one goal to be attained!

Affix to the Upanishad, the bow incomparable, the sharp arrow of devotional worship; then, with mind absorbed and heart melted in love, draw the arrow and hit the mark—the imperishable Brahman.

OM is the bow, the arrow is the individual being, and Brahman is the target. With a tranquil heart, take aim. Lose thyself in him, even as the arrow is lost in the target.

In him are woven heaven, earth, and sky, together with the mind and all the senses. Know him, the Self alone. Give up vain talk. He is the bridge of immortality.

Within the lotus of the heart he dwells, where, like the spokes of a wheel, the nerves meet. Meditate on him as OM. Easily mayest thou cross the sea of darkness.

This Self, who understands all, who knows all, and whose glory is manifest in the universe, lives within the lotus of the heart, the bright throne of Brahman.

By the pure in heart is he known. The Self exists in man, within the lotus of the heart, and is the master of his life and of his body. With mind illumined by the power of meditation, the wise know him, the blissful, the immortal.

The knot of the heart, which is ignorance, is loosed, all doubts are dissolved, all evil effects of deeds are destroyed, when he who is both personal and impersonal is realized.

In the effulgent lotus of the heart dwells Brahman, who is passionless and indivisible. He is pure, he is the light of lights. Him the knowers of the Self attain.

Him the sun does not illumine, nor the moon, nor the stars, nor the lightning—nor, verily, fires kindled upon earth. He is the one light that gives light to all. He shining, everything shines.

This immortal Brahman is before, this immortal Brahman is behind, this immortal Brahman extends to the right and to the left, above and below. Verily, all is Brahman, and Brahman is supreme.

Like two birds of golden plumage, inseparable companions, the individual self and the immortal Self are perched on the branches of the

selfsame tree. The former tastes of the sweet and
bitter fruits of the tree; the latter, tasting of
neither, calmly observes.

The individual self, deluded by forgetfulness
of his identity with the divine Self, bewildered
by his ego, grieves and is sad. But when he recog-
nizes the worshipful Lord as his own true Self,
and beholds his glory, he grieves no more.

When the seer beholds the Effulgent One, the
Lord, the Supreme Being, then, transcending both
good and evil, and freed from impurities, he unites
himself with him.

The Lord is the one life shining forth from
every creature. Seeing him present in all, the wise
man is humble, puts not himself forward. His
delight is in the Self, his joy is in the Self, he
serves the Lord in all. Such as he, indeed, are the
true knowers of Brahman.

This Effulgent Self is to be realized within the
lotus of the heart by continence, by steadfastness
in truth and meditation, and by superconscious
vision. Their impurities washed away, the seers
realize him.

Truth alone succeeds, not untruth. By truthfulness the path of felicity is opened up, the path
which is taken by the sages, freed from cravings,
and which leads them to truth's eternal abode.

Brahman is supreme; he is self-luminous, he is

beyond all thought. Subtler than the subtlest is he, farther than the farthest, nearer than the nearest. He resides in the lotus of the heart of every being.

The eyes do not see him, speech cannot utter him, the senses cannot reach him. He is to be attained neither by austerity nor by sacrificial rites. When through discrimination the heart has become pure, then, in meditation, the Impersonal Self is revealed.

The subtle Self within the living and breathing body is realized in that pure consciousness wherein is no duality—that consciousness by which the heart beats and the senses perform their office.

Whether of heaven, or of heavenly enjoyments, whether of desires, or of objects of desire, whatever thought arises in the heart of the sage is fulfilled. Therefore let him who seeks his own good revere and worship the sage.

The sage knows Brahman, the support of all, the pure effulgent being in whom is contained the universe. They who worship the sage, and do so without thought of self, cross the boundary of birth and death.

He who, brooding upon sense objects, comes to yearn for them, is born here and there, again and again, driven by his desire. But he who has realized the Self, and thus satisfied all hunger, attains to liberation even in this life.

The Self is not to be known through study of
the scriptures, nor through subtlety of the intellect, nor through much learning. But by him
who longs for him is he known. Verily unto him
does the Self reveal his true being.

The Self is not to be known by the weak, nor
by the thoughtless, nor by those who do not
rightly meditate. But by the rightly meditative,
the thoughtful, and the strong, he is fully known.

Having known the Self, the sages are filled with
joy. Blessed are they, tranquil of mind, free from
passion. Realizing everywhere the all-pervading
Brahman, deeply absorbed in contemplation of his
being, they enter into him, the Self of all.

Having fully ascertained and realized the truth
of Vedanta, having established themselves in purity of conduct by following the yoga of renunciation, these great ones attain to immortality in
this very life; and when their bodies fall away
from them at death, they attain to liberation.

When death overtakes the body, the vital energy
enters the cosmic source, the senses dissolve in their
cause, and karmas and the individual soul are lost
in Brahman, the pure, the changeless, the infinite.

As rivers flow into the sea and in so doing lose
name and form, even so the wise man, freed from
name and form, attains the Supreme Being, the
Self-Luminous, the Infinite.

He who knows Brahman becomes Brahman. No one ignorant of Brahman is ever born in his family. He passes beyond all sorrow. He overcomes evil. Freed from the fetters of ignorance, he becomes immortal.

Let the truth of Brahman be taught only to those who obey his law, who are devoted to him, and who are pure in heart. To the impure let it never be taught.

Hail to the sages! Hail to the illumined souls!

This truth of Brahman was taught in ancient times to Shounaka by Angira. Hail to the sages! Hail to the illumined souls!

OM . . . Peace—peace—peace.

VI

MANDUKYA

THE life of man is divided between waking, dreaming, and dreamless sleep. But transcending these three states is superconscious vision—called simply The Fourth.

MANDUKYA

OM . . .
With our ears may we hear what is good.
With our eyes may we behold thy righteousness.
Tranquil in body, may we who worship thee find rest.
OM . . . Peace—peace—peace.

THE SYLLABLE OM, which is the imperishable Brahman, is the universe. Whatsoever has existed, whatsoever exists, whatsoever shall exist hereafter, is OM. And whatsoever transcends past, present, and future, that also is OM.

All this that we see without is Brahman. This Self that is within is Brahman.

This Self, which is one with OM, has three aspects, and beyond these three, different from them and indefinable—The Fourth.

The first aspect of the Self is the universal person, the collective symbol of created beings, in his physical nature—Vaiswanara. He is awake, and is conscious only of external objects. He has seven members. The heavens are his head, the sun his eyes, air his breath, fire his heart, water his belly, earth his feet, and space his body. He has nineteen instruments of knowledge: five organs of

sense, five organs of action, five functions of the
breath, together with mind, intellect, heart, and
ego. He is the enjoyer of the pleasures of sense.

The second aspect of the Self is the universal
person in his mental nature—Taijasa. He has
seven members and nineteen instruments of knowledge. He is dreaming, and is conscious only of his
dreams. In this state he is the enjoyer of the subtle
impressions in the mind of the deeds he has done
in the past.

The third aspect of the Self is the universal person in dreamless sleep—Prajna. He dreams not.
He is without desire. As the darkness of night
covers the day, and the visible world seems to
disappear, so in dreamless sleep the veil of unconsciousness envelops his thought and knowledge,
and the subtle impressions of his mind apparently
vanish. Since he experiences neither strife nor anx-
iety, he is said to be blissful, and the experiencer
of bliss.

Prajna is the lord of all. He knows all things.
He is the dweller in the hearts of all. He is the
origin of all. He is the end of all.[1]

---

[1] The Prajna is known as Iswara, or God in his personal
aspect. Dreamless sleep is ignorance. Within this ignorance
exist all the three states of consciousness: the waking state,
the dream state, and the state of dreamless sleep. Iswara,
technically, is Brahman associated with Maya, or universal

The Fourth, say the wise, is not subjective experience, nor objective experience, nor experience intermediate between these two, nor is it a negative condition which is neither consciousness nor unconsciousness. It is not the knowledge of the senses, nor is it relative knowledge, nor yet inferential knowledge. Beyond the senses, beyond the understanding, beyond all expression, is The Fourth. It is pure unitary consciousness, wherein awareness of the world and of multiplicity is completely obliterated. It is ineffable peace. It is the supreme good. It is One without a second. It is the Self. Know it alone!

This Self, beyond all words, is the syllable OM. This syllable, though indivisible, consists of three letters—A-U-M.

Vaiswanara, the Self as the universal person in his physical being, corresponds to the first letter—A. Whosoever knows Vaiswanara obtains what he desires, and becomes the first among men.

Taijasa, the Self as the universal person in his mental being, corresponds to the second letter—U. Taijasa and the letter U both stand in dream,

ignorance, and the individual man is Brahman associated with individual ignorance. The distinction between God and man is that God controls ignorance, man is controlled by it.

between waking and sleeping. Whosoever knows
Taijasa grows in wisdom, and is highly honored.

Prajna, the Self as the universal person in
dreamless sleep, corresponds to the third letter—M.
He is the origin and the end of all. Whosoever
knows Prajna knows all things.

The Fourth, the Self, is OM, the indivisible
syllable. This syllable is unutterable, and beyond
mind. In it the manifold universe disappears. It
is the supreme good—One without a second.
Whosoever knows OM, the Self, becomes the Self.

VII

TAITTIRIYA

MAN, in his ignorance, identifies himself with the material sheaths that encompass his true Self. Transcending these, he becomes one with Brahman, who is pure bliss.

TAITTIRIYA

OM . . .
May Mitra grant us peace!
May Varuna grant us peace!
May Aryama grant us peace!
May Indra and Brihaspati grant us peace!
May the all-pervading Vishnu grant us peace!
Hail to Brahman!
Hail to thee, thou source of all power!

THOU ART indeed the manifested Brahman. Of thee will I speak. Thee will I proclaim in my thoughts as true. Thee will I proclaim on my lips as true.

May truth protect me, may it protect my teacher, may it protect us both. May glory come to us both. May the light of Brahman shine in us both.

Thou art Brahman, one with the syllable OM, which is in all scriptures—the supreme syllable, the mother of all sound. Do thou strengthen me with true wisdom. May I, O Lord, realize the Immortal. May my body be strong and whole; may my tongue be sweet; may my ears hear only praise of thee. The syllable OM is verily thine

image. Through this syllable thou mayest be attained. Thou art beyond the grasp of the intellect.
Vouchsafe that I forget not what I have learned
in the scriptures.

Thou art the source of all happiness and of all
prosperity. Do thou come to me as the goddess
of prosperity and shower thy blessings upon me.

May the seekers after truth gather round me,
may they come from everywhere, that I may teach
them thy word.

May I be a glory among men. May I be richer
than the richest. May I enter into thee, O Lord;
and mayest thou reveal thyself unto me. Purified
am I by thy touch, O Lord of manifold forms.

Thou art the refuge of those who surrender
themselves to thee. Reveal thyself to me. Make
me thine own. I take my refuge in thee.

Thou art the Lord, immortal, self-luminous,
and of golden effulgence, within the lotus of every
heart. Within the heart art thou revealed to those
that seek thee.

He who dwells in thee becomes king over himself. He controls his wandering thoughts. He becomes master of his speech and of all his organs
of sense. He becomes master of his intellect.

Thou art Brahman, whose form is invisible,
like ether; whose Self is truth. Thou art perfect

peace and immortality, the solace of life, the delight of the mind. May I worship thee!

OM is Brahman. OM is all. He who meditates
on OM attains to Brahman.

Having attained to Brahman, a sage declared:
"I am life. My glory is like the mountain peak.
I am established in the purity of Brahman. I have
attained the freedom of the Self. I am Brahman,
self-luminous, the brightest treasure. I am endowed with wisdom. I am immortal, imperishable."

OM . . . Peace—peace—peace.

To a Lay Student

Let your conduct be marked by right action,
including study and teaching of the scriptures; by
truthfulness in word, deed, and thought; by self-
denial and the practice of austerity; by poise and
self-control; by performance of the everyday du-
ties of life with a cheerful heart and an unattached
mind.

Speak the truth. Do your duty. Do not neglect
the study of the scriptures. Do not cut the thread
of progeny. Swerve not from truth. Deviate not
from the path of good. Revere greatness.

Let your mother be a god to you; let your
father be a god to you; let your teacher be a god

to you; let your guest also be a god to you. Do only such actions as are blameless. Always show reverence to the great.

Whatever you give to others, give with love and reverence. Gifts must be given in abundance, with joy, humility, and compassion.

If at any time there is any doubt with regard to right conduct, follow the practice of great souls, who are guileless, of good judgment, and devoted to truth.

Thus conduct yourself always. This is the injunction, this is the teaching, and this is the command of the scriptures.

He who knows Brahman attains the supreme goal. Brahman is the abiding reality, he is pure knowledge, and he is infinity. He who knows that Brahman dwells within the lotus of the heart becomes one with him and enjoys all blessings.

Out of Brahman, who is the Self, came ether; out of ether, air; out of air, fire; out of fire, water; out of water, earth; out of earth, vegetation; out of vegetation, food; out of food, the body of man. The body of man, composed of the essence of food, is the physical sheath of the Self.

From food are born all creatures, which live upon food and after death return to food. Food is the chief of all things. It is therefore said to be medicine for all diseases of the body. Those who

worship food as Brahman gain all material objects. From food are born all beings which, being
born, grow by food. All beings feed upon food,
and, when they die, food feeds upon them.

Different from the physical sheath is the vital
sheath. This is encased in the physical sheath and
has the same form. Through this the senses perform their office. From this men and beasts derive
their life. This determines the length of life of all
creatures. He who worships the vital sheath as
Brahman lives to complete his span of life. This
sheath is the living self of the physical sheath.

Different from the vital sheath is the mental
sheath. This is encased in the vital sheath and has
the same form.

Words cannot express the bliss of Brahman,
mind cannot reach it. The sage, who knows it, is
freed from fear.

The mental sheath is the living self of the vital
sheath.

Different from the mental sheath is the intellectual sheath. This is encased in the mental sheath
and has the same form.

All actions, sacrificial or otherwise, are performed through the intellect. All the senses pay
homage to the intellectual sheath. He who worships intellect as Brahman does not err; he does

not identify himself with the other sheaths, and does not yield to the passions of the body.

Different from the intellectual sheath is the sheath of the ego. This sheath is encased in the intellectual sheath and has the same form.

Beyond all sheaths is the Self.

Vain and useless becomes his life who thinks of Brahman as nonexistent. He alone who knows Brahman as existent truly lives.

Surely at death a foolish man does not attain Brahman, but only a wise man.

Desiring that he should become many, that he should make of himself many forms, Brahman meditated. Meditating, he created all things.

Creating all things, he entered into everything. Entering into all things, he became that which has shape and that which is shapeless; he became that which can be defined and that which cannot be defined; he became that which has support and that which has not support; he became that which is conscious and that which is not conscious; he became that which is gross and that which is subtle. He became all things whatsoever: therefore the wise call him the Real.

Concerning which truth it is written: *Before creation came into existence, Brahman existed as the Unmanifest. From the Unmanifest was created*

the manifest. From himself he brought forth him-
self. Hence he is known as the Self-Existent.

The Self-Existent is the essence of all felicity.
Who could live, who could breathe, if that blissful
Self dwelt not within the lotus of the heart? He
it is that gives joy.

When a man finds his existence and unity in
the Self—who is the basis of life, who is beyond
the senses, who is formless, inexpressible, beyond
all predicates—then alone does he transcend fear.
So long as there is the least idea of separation from
him, there is fear. To the man who thinks himself
learned, yet knows not himself as Brahman, Brahman, who drives away all fear, appears as fear
itself.

Concerning which truth it is written: *Through*
fear of Brahman the wind blows and the sun
shines; through fear of him Indra, the god of
rain, Agni, the god of fire, and Yama, the god of
death, perform their tasks.

Who could live, who could breathe, if that
blissful Self dwelt not within the lotus of the
heart? He it is that gives joy.

Of what nature is this joy?

Consider the lot of a young man, noble, well-
read, intelligent, strong, healthy, with all the
wealth of the world at his command. Assume that
he is happy, and measure his joy as one unit.

One hundred times that joy is one unit of the joy of Gandharvas: but no less joy than Gandharvas has the seer to whom the Self has been revealed, and who is without craving.[1]

One hundred times the joy of Gandharvas is one unit of the joy of celestial Gandharvas: but no less joy than celestial Gandharvas has the sage to whom the Self has been revealed, and who is without craving.

One hundred times the joy of celestial Gandharvas is one unit of the joy of the Pitris in their paradise: but no less joy than the Pitris in their paradise has the sage to whom the Self has been revealed, and who is without craving.

One hundred times the joy of the Pitris in their paradise is one unit of the joy of the Devas: but no less joy than the Devas has the sage to whom the Self has been revealed, and who is without craving.

One hundred times the joy of the Devas is one unit of the joy of the karma Devas: but no less joy than the karma Devas has the sage to whom the Self has been revealed, and who is without craving.

One hundred times the joy of the karma Devas

[1] Gandharvas, Pitris, Devas, etc., are beings of a higher order than man. According to the Upanishads, here and elsewhere, many worlds, inhabited by various beings, make up the universe.

is one unit of the joy of the ruling Devas: but
no less joy than the ruling Devas has the sage
to whom the Self has been revealed, and who is
without craving.

One hundred times the joy of the ruling Devas
is one unit of the joy of Indra: but no less joy
than Indra has the sage to whom the Self has been
revealed, and who is without craving.

One hundred times the joy of Indra is one unit
of the joy of Brihaspati: but no less joy than
Brihaspati has the sage to whom the Self has been
revealed, and who is without craving.

One hundred times the joy of Brihaspati is one
unit of the joy of Prajapati: but no less joy than
Prajapati has the sage to whom the Self has been
revealed, and who is without craving.

One hundred times the joy of Prajapati is one
unit of the joy of Brahma: but no less joy than
Brahma has the seer to whom the Self has been
revealed, and who is without craving.

He who is the Self in man, and he who is the
Self in the sun, are one. Verily, he who knows
this truth overcomes the world; he transcends the
physical sheath, he transcends the vital sheath, he
transcends the mental sheath, he transcends the
intellectual sheath, he transcends the sheath of the
ego.

It is written: *He who knows the joy of Brah-*

man, which words cannot express and the mind cannot reach, is free from fear. He is not distressed by the thought, "Why did I not do what is right? Why did I do what is wrong?" He who knows the joy of Brahman, knowing both good and evil, transcends both.

OM . . .

May Brahman protect us, may he guide us, may he give us strength and right understanding.

May peace and love be with us all!

Bhrigu, respectfully approaching his father Varuna, said: "Sir, teach me Brahman." Varuna explained to him the physical sheath and the vital sheath and the functions of the senses, and added: "He from whom all beings are born, in whom they live, being born, and to whom at death they return—seek to know him. He is Brahman."

Bhrigu practiced austerity and meditation. Then it seemed to him that food was Brahman. For of food all beings are born, by food they are sustained, being born, and into food they enter after death.

This knowledge, however, did not satisfy him. He again approached his father Varuna and said: "Sir, teach me Brahman."

Varuna replied: "Seek to know Brahman by meditation. Meditation is Brahman."

Bhrigu practiced meditation and learned that primal energy is Brahman. For from primal energy all beings are born, by primal energy they are sustained, being born, and into primal energy they enter after death.

But Bhrigu was still doubtful about his knowledge. So he approached his father again and said: "Sir, teach me Brahman." Varuna replied: "Seek to know Brahman by meditation. Meditation is Brahman."

Bhrigu practiced meditation and learned that mind is Brahman. For from mind all beings are born, by mind they are sustained, being born, and into mind they enter after death.

Still doubtful, he approached his father and said: "Sir, teach me Brahman." His father replied: "Seek to know Brahman by meditation. Meditation is Brahman."

Bhrigu practiced meditation and learned that intellect is Brahman. For from intellect all beings are born, by intellect they are sustained, being born, and into intellect they return after death.

Not yet satisfied, doubting his understanding, Bhrigu approached his father and said: "Sir, teach me Brahman." Varuna replied: "Seek to know Brahman by meditation. Meditation is Brahman."

Bhrigu practiced meditation and learned that joy is Brahman. For from joy all beings are born, by joy they are sustained, being born, and into joy they enter after death.

This is the wisdom which Bhrigu, taught by Varuna, attained within his heart.

He who attains this wisdom wins glory, grows rich, enjoys health and fame.

Brahman is to be meditated upon as the source of all thought and life and action. He is the splendor in wealth, he is the light in the stars. He is all things.

Let a man meditate upon Brahman as support, and he will be supported. Let him meditate upon Brahman as greatness, and he will be great. Let him meditate upon Brahman as mind, and he will be endowed with intellectual power. Let him meditate upon Brahman as adoration, and he will be adored. Let him worship Brahman as Brahman, and he will become Brahman.

He who is the Self in man, and he who is the Self in the sun, are one.

I am that Self! I am life immortal! I overcome

the world—I who am endowed with golden effulgence! Those who know me achieve Reality.

OM . . . Peace—peace—peace.

VIII

AITAREYA

BRAHMAN, source, sustenance, and end of the universe, partakes of every phase of existence. He wakes with the waking man, dreams with the dreamer, and sleeps the deep sleep of the dreamless sleeper; but he transcends these three states to become himself. His true nature is pure consciousness.

AITAREYA

*May my speech be one with my mind, and may my
    mind be one with my speech.*
*O thou self-luminous Brahman, remove the veil of
    ignorance from before me, that I may behold thy
    light.*
Do thou reveal to me the spirit of the scriptures.
May the truth of the scriptures be ever present to me.
*May I seek day and night to realize what I learn from
    the sages.*
May I speak the truth of Brahman.
May I speak the truth.
May it protect me.
May it protect my teacher.
OM . . . Peace—peace—peace.

BEFORE CREATION, all that existed was the Self,
the Self alone. Nothing else was. Then the Self
thought: "Let me send forth the worlds."

He sent forth these worlds: *Ambhas,* the highest world, above the sky and upheld by it; *Marichi,*
the sky; *Mara,* the mortal world, the earth; and
Apa, the world beneath the earth.

He thought: "Behold the worlds. Let me now
send forth their guardians." Then he sent forth
their guardians.

He thought: "Behold these worlds and the

guardians of these worlds. Let me send forth food for the guardians." Then he sent forth food for them.

He thought: "How shall there be guardians and I have no part in them?

"If, without me, speech utters, breath is drawn, eye sees, ear hears, skin feels, mind thinks, sex organs procreate, then what am I?"

He thought: "Let me enter the guardians." Whereupon, opening the center of their skulls, he entered. The door by which he entered is called the door of bliss.[1]

The Self being unknown, all three states of the soul are but dreaming—waking, dreaming, and dreamless sleep. In each of these dwells the Self: the eye is his dwelling place while we wake, the mind is his dwelling place while we dream, the lotus of the heart is his dwelling place while we sleep the dreamless sleep.

Having entered into the guardians, he identified himself with them. He became many individual beings. Now, therefore, if an individual awakes

---

[1] The sages declare that this door of bliss, the highest center of spiritual consciousness, technically known as the Sahashrara, the thousand-petaled lotus, is situated in the center of the brain. When the yogi's mind, absorbed in meditation, reaches this center, he realizes his unity with Brahman.

from his threefold dream of waking, dreaming,
and dreamless sleep, he sees no other than the Self.
He sees the Self dwelling in the lotus of his heart
as Brahman, omnipresent, and he declares: "I
know Brahman!" [1]

Who is this Self whom we desire to worship?
Of what nature is this Self?

Is he the self by which we see form, hear sound,
smell odor, speak words, and taste the sweet or
the bitter?

Is he the heart and the mind by which we
perceive, command, discriminate, know, think, remember, will, feel, desire, breathe, love, and perform other like acts?

Nay, these are but adjuncts of the Self, who
is pure consciousness. And this Self, who is pure
consciousness, is Brahman. He is God, all gods;
the five elements—earth, air, fire, water, ether;
all beings, great or small, born of eggs, born from
the womb, born from heat, born from soil; horses,
cows, men, elephants, birds; everything that
breathes, the beings that walk and the beings that
walk not. The reality behind all these is Brahman,
who is pure consciousness.

[1] The Mandukya Upanishad designates this experience as
"The Fourth," transcending the three states and differing
from them in kind.

All these, while they live, and after they have ceased to live, exist in him.

The sage Vamadeva, having realized Brahman as pure consciousness, departed this life, ascended into heaven, obtained all his desires, and achieved immortality.

IX

CHANDOGYA

BRAHMAN is all. From Brahman come appearances, sensations, desires, deeds. But all these are merely name and form. To know Brahman one must experience the identity between him and the Self, or Brahman dwelling within the lotus of the heart. Only by so doing can man escape from sorrow and death, and become one with the subtle essence beyond all knowledge.

CHANDOGYA

May quietness descend upon my limbs,
My speech, my breath, my eyes, my ears;
May all my senses wax clear and strong.
May Brahman show himself unto me.
May I never deny Brahman, nor Brahman me.
I with him and he with me—may we abide always
*   together.*
May there be revealed to me,
Who am devoted to Brahman,
The holy truth of the Upanishads.
OM . . . Peace—peace—peace.

THE REQUIREMENTS of duty are three. The first is sacrifice, study, almsgiving; the second is austerity; the third is life as a student in the home of a teacher and the practice of continence. Together, these three lead one to the realm of the blest. But he who is firmly established in the knowledge of Brahman achieves immortality.

The light that shines above the heavens and above this world, the light that shines in the highest world, beyond which there are no others—that is the light that shines in the hearts of men.

Truly has this universe come forth from Brahman. In Brahman it lives and has its being. Assuredly, all is Brahman. Let a man, freed from the taint of passion, worship Brahman alone.

A man is, above all, his will. As is his will in this life, so does he become when he departs from it. Therefore should his will be fixed on attaining Brahman.

The Self, who is to be realized by the purified mind and the illumined consciousness, whose form is light, whose thoughts are true; who, like the ether, remains pure and unattached; from whom proceed all works, all desires, all odors, all tastes; who pervades all, who is beyond the senses, and in whom there is fullness of joy forever—he is my very Self, dwelling within the lotus of my heart.

Smaller than a grain of rice is the Self; smaller than a grain of barley, smaller than a mustard seed, smaller than a canary seed, yea, smaller even than the kernel of a canary seed. Yet again is that Self, within the lotus of my heart, greater than the earth, greater than the heavens, yea, greater than all the worlds.

He from whom proceed all works, all desires, all odors, all tastes; who pervades all, who is beyond the senses, and in whom there is fullness of joy forever—he, the heart-enshrined Self, is verily Brahman. I, who worship the Self within the lotus of my heart, will attain him at death.

He who worships him, and puts his trust in him, shall surely attain him.

Said the seer Sandilya: At the moment of death a knower of Brahman should meditate on the following truths:

> *Thou art imperishable.*
> *Thou art the changeless Reality.*
> *Thou art the source of life.*

This highest knowledge, the knowledge of Brahman, having drunk of which one never thirsts, did Ghora Angirasa teach to Krishna, the son of Devaki.

One day the boy Satyakama came to his mother and said: "Mother, I want to be a religious student. What is my family name?"

"My son," replied his mother, "I do not know. In my youth I was a servant and worked in many places. I do not know who was your father. I am Jabala, and you are Satyakama. Call yourself Satyakama Jabala."

Thereupon the boy went to Gautama and asked to be accepted as a student. "Of what family are you, my lad?" inquired the sage.

Satyakama replied: "I asked my mother what my family name was, and she answered: 'I do not know. In my youth I was a servant and

worked in many places. I do not know who was
your father. I am Jabala, and you are Satyakama.
Call yourself Satyakama Jabala!' I am therefore
Satyakama Jabala, sir."

Then said the sage: "None but a true Brahmin
would have spoken thus. Go and fetch fuel, for
I will teach you. You have not swerved from the
truth."

After initiating Satyakama, the sage gave him
four hundred lean and sickly cattle, saying, "Take
good care of these, my lad." The boy promptly
drove them toward the forest, vowing to himself
that he would not return until they numbered
a thousand. He dwelt in the forest for many
years, and when the cattle had increased to a
thousand, the bull of the herd approached him and
said: "Satyakama, we have become a herd of one
thousand. Do you now lead us to the house of
your master, and I will teach you one foot of
Brahman."

"Speak out, please," said Satyakama.

Then said the bull: "The east is a part of the
Lord, and so is the west; the south is a part of the
Lord, and so is the north. The four cardinal
points form a foot of Brahman. Fire will teach
you another."

On the following day Satyakama began his
journey. Toward evening he lighted a fire, and as

he sat down facing the east to worship he heard
a voice from the fire saying, "Satyakama, I will
teach you one foot of Brahman. This earth is a
portion of Brahman. The sky and the heavens
are portions of him. The ocean is a portion of him.
All these form a foot of Brahman. A swan will
teach you another."

Satyakama continued his journey. On the following evening, when he had lighted his fire and
seated himself facing the east to worship, a swan
flew to him and said: "I have come to teach you
one foot of Brahman. This lighted fire before
you, O Satyakama, is a part of Brahman, and likewise the moon; the lightning, too, is a part. All
these form a foot of Brahman. A loon will teach
you another."

The next evening, as Satyakama lighted his fire
and seated himself facing the east to worship, a
loon came near him and said: "I will teach you
one foot of Brahman. Breath is a part of Brahman, sight is a part of Brahman, hearing is a
part of Brahman, mind is a part of Brahman. All
these form a foot of Brahman."

At last the youth arrived at the home of his
master and reverently presented himself before
him. As soon as Gautama saw him, he exclaimed:
"My son, your face shines like a knower of Brahman. By whom were you taught?"

"By beings other than men," replied Satya-kama; "but I desire that you too should teach me. For I have heard from the wise that the knowledge that the Guru imparts will alone lead to the supreme good."

Then the sage taught him that knowledge, and left nothing out.

Upakosala dwelt as a student in the house of Satyakama for twelve years. Though the teacher let other disciples return to their homes after they had been duly taught the way of truth, Upako-sala was not allowed to depart. The wife of Satyakama entreated her husband to finish teaching him in order that he might go home like the rest, but Satyakama not only refused to do so but went off on a journey. At this Upakosala was so sad and sick at heart that he could not eat. The teacher's wife plied him with food, and in everything treated him with tender affection, but to no avail. At last the boy cried out to her: "O mother, my heart is still so impure; I am too unhappy to eat!"

Then a voice from out the fire which he was tending said: "This life is Brahman. The sky is Brahman. Bliss is Brahman. Know thou Brahman!"

"I know that life is Brahman," replied Upakosala. "But that the sky is Brahman, or that bliss is Brahman, I do not know."

Again came the voice from out the fire, this time explaining that by sky was meant the lotus of the heart, wherein dwells Brahman, and that by bliss was meant the bliss of Brahman. "Both," said the voice, "refer to Brahman"; and, continuing, it taught Upakosala thus:

"Earth, food, fire, sun—all these that you worship—are forms of Brahman. He who is seen in the sun—that one am I. He who dwells in the east, in the north, in the west, and in the south, he who dwells in the moon, in the stars, and in water— that one am I. He who dwells in the sky and makes the lightning his home—that one also am I. Know well the true nature of the world that it may never do you harm."

Thereupon the fire, which had been only an earthly fire with which to prepare sacrifices, assumed a new aspect, and became the Lord himself. The earth was transformed; life was transformed; the sun, the moon, the stars, the lightning—everything was transformed, and deified. And thus it was that to Upakosala the true nature of all things was revealed.

In due time Satyakama returned home. When he saw Upakosala, he said:

"My son, your face shines like one who knows Brahman. Who has taught you?"

"Beings other than men," replied Upakosala.

Then said Satyakama: "My son, what you have learned is true. True also is this that I teach you now. Lo, to him who knows it shall no evil cling, even as drops of water cling not to the leaf of the lotus:

"He who glows in the depths of your eyes— that is Brahman; that is the Self of yourself. He is the Beautiful One, he is the Luminous One. In all the worlds, forever and ever, he shines!"

When Svetaketu was twelve years old, his father Uddalaka said to him, "Svetaketu, you must now go to school and study. None of our family, my child, is ignorant of Brahman."

Thereupon Svetaketu went to a teacher and studied for twelve years. After committing to memory all the Vedas, he returned home full of pride in his learning.

His father, noticing the young man's conceit, said to him: "Svetaketu, have you asked for that knowledge by which we hear the unhearable, by which we perceive the unperceivable, by which we know the unknowable?"

"What is that knowledge, sir?" asked Svetaketu.

"My child, as by knowing one lump of clay, all things made of clay are known, the difference being only in name and arising from speech, and the truth being that all are clay; as by knowing a nugget of gold, all things made of gold are known, the difference being only in name and arising from speech, and the truth being that all are gold—exactly so is that knowledge, knowing which we know all."

"But surely those venerable teachers of mine are ignorant of this knowledge; for if they possessed it, they would have taught it to me. Do you therefore, sir, give me that knowledge."

"Be it so," said Uddalaka, and continued thus:

"In the beginning there was Existence, One only, without a second. Some say that in the beginning there was non-existence only, and that out of that the universe was born. But how could such a thing be? How could existence be born of non-existence? No, my son, in the beginning there was Existence alone—One only, without a second. He, the One, thought to himself: Let me be many, let me grow forth. Thus out of himself he projected the universe: and having projected out of himself the universe, he entered into every being and every thing. All that is has its self in him alone. He is the truth. He is the subtle essence of all. He is the Self. And that, Svetaketu, THAT ART THOU."

"Please, sir, tell me more about this Self."

"Be it so, my child:

"As the bees make honey by gathering juices from many flowering plants and trees, and as these juices reduced to one honey do not know from what flowers they severally come, similarly, my son, all creatures, when they are merged in that one Existence, whether in dreamless sleep or in death, know nothing of their past or present state, because of the ignorance enveloping them——know not that they are merged in him and that from him they came.

"Whatever these creatures are, whether a lion, or a tiger, or a boar, or a worm, or a gnat, or a mosquito, that they remain after they come back from dreamless sleep.

"All these have their self in him alone. He is the truth. He is the subtle essence of all. He is the Self. And that, Svetaketu, THAT ART THOU."

"Please, sir, tell me more about this Self."

"Be it so, my son:

"The rivers in the east flow eastward, the rivers in the west flow westward, and all enter into the sea. From sea to sea they pass, the clouds lifting them to the sky as vapor and sending them down as rain. And as these rivers, when they are united

with the sea, do not know whether they are this or
that river, likewise all those creatures that I have
named, when they have come back from Brahman,
know not whence they came.

"All those beings have their self in him alone.
He is the truth. He is the subtle essence of all.
He is the Self. And that, Svetaketu, THAT ART
THOU."

"Please, sir, tell me more about this Self."

"Be it so, my child:

"If someone were to strike once at the root of
this large tree, it would bleed, but live. If he were
to strike at its stem, it would bleed, but live. If
he were to strike at the top, it would bleed, but
live. Pervaded by the living self, this tree stands
firm, and takes its food; but if the Self were to
depart from one of its branches, that branch
would wither; if it were to depart from a second,
that would wither; if it were to depart from a
third, that would wither. If it were to depart
from the whole tree, the whole tree would wither.

"Likewise, my son, know this: The body dies
when the Self leaves it—but the Self dies not.

"All that is has its self in him alone. He is the
truth. He is the subtle essence of all. He is the Self.
And that, Svetaketu, THAT ART THOU."

"Please, sir, tell me more about this Self."

"Be it so. Bring a fruit of that Nyagrodha tree."

"Here it is, sir."

"Break it."

"It is broken, sir."

"What do you see?"

"Some seeds, extremely small, sir."

"Break one of them."

"It is broken, sir."

"What do you see?"

"Nothing, sir."

"The subtle essence you do not see, and in that is the whole of the Nyagrodha tree. Believe, my son, that that which is the subtle essence—in that have all things their existence. That is the truth. That is the Self. And that, Svetaketu, THAT ART THOU."

"Please, sir, tell me more about this Self."

"Be it so. Put this salt in water, and come to me tomorrow morning."

Svetaketu did as he was bidden. The next morning his father asked him to bring the salt which he had put in the water. But he could not, for it had dissolved. Then said Uddalaka:

"Sip the water, and tell me how it tastes."

"It is salty, sir."

"In the same way," continued Uddalaka, "though you do not see Brahman in this body, he is indeed here. That which is the subtle essence —in that have all things their existence. That

is the truth. That is the Self. And that, Svetaketu,
THAT ART THOU."

"Please, sir, tell me more about this Self," said
the youth again.

"Be it so, my child:

"As a man may be blindfolded, and led away,
and left in a strange place; and as, having been so
dealt with, he turns in every direction and cries
out for someone to remove his bandages and show
him the way home; and as one thus entreated
may loose his bandages and give him comfort;
and as thereupon he walks from village to village,
asking his way as he goes; and as he arrives home
at last—just so does a man who meets with an
illumined teacher obtain true knowledge.

"That which is the subtle essence—in that have
all beings their existence. That is the truth. That is
the Self. And that, O Svetaketu, THAT ART
THOU."

"Please, sir, tell me more about this Self."

"Be it so, my child:

"When a man is fatally ill, his relations gather
round him and ask, 'Do you know me? Do you
know me?' Now until his speech is merged in
his mind, his mind in his breath, his breath in his
vital heat, his vital heat in the Supreme Being,
he knows them. But when his speech is merged in
his mind, his mind in his breath, his breath in his

vital heat, his vital heat in the Supreme Being, then he does not know them.

"That which is the subtle essence—in that have all beings their existence. That is the truth. That is the Self. And that, O Svetaketu, THAT ART THOU."

Narada once came to Sanatkumara and asked to be taught. To Sanatkumara's question, "What have you already studied?" Narada replied that he had studied all the branches of learning—art, science, music, and philosophy, as well as the sacred scriptures. "But," said he, "I have gained no peace. I have studied all this, but the Self I do not know. I have heard from great teachers like you that he who knows the Self overcomes grief. Grief is ever my lot. Help me, I pray you, to overcome it."

Sanatkumara said: "Whatever you have read is only name. Meditate on name as Brahman."

Narada asked: "Is there anything higher than name?"

"Yes, speech is higher than name. It is through speech that we come to know the many branches of learning, that we come to know what is right and what is wrong, what is true and what is untrue, what is good and what is bad, what is pleasant and what is unpleasant. For if there were no

speech, neither right nor wrong would be known,
neither the true nor the false, neither the good nor
the bad, neither the pleasant nor the unpleasant.
Speech makes us know all this. Meditate on speech
as Brahman."

"Sir, is there anything higher than speech?"

"Yes, mind is higher than speech. As the closed
fist holds two amalaka fruits or two kola fruits
or two aksha fruits, so does mind hold name and
speech. For if a man thinks in his mind to study
the sacred hymns, he studies them; if he thinks
in his mind to do certain deeds, he does them; if
he thinks in his mind to gain family and wealth,
he gains them; if he thinks in his mind to be
happy in this world and the next, he is happy,
here and there. Mind is the chief inner organ of
the Self. Mind is the means to happiness. Meditate on mind as Brahman."

"Sir, is there anything higher than mind?"

"Yes, will is higher than mind. For when a
man wills, he thinks in his mind; and when he
thinks in his mind, he puts forth speech; and when
he puts forth speech, he clothes his speech in words.
All these, therefore, center in will, consist of will,
and abide in will. Meditate on will as Brahman."

"Sir, is there anything higher than will?"

"Yes, discriminating will is higher than will.
For when a man discriminates by analyzing his

past experiences and considering on the basis of these what may come in the future, he rightly wills in the present. Meditate on discriminating will as Brahman."

"Sir, is there anything higher than discriminating will?"

"Yes, concentration is higher than discriminating will. Those who reach greatness here on earth reach it through concentration. Thus, while small and vulgar people are always gossiping and quarrelling and for lack of concentration abusing one another, great men, possessing it, obtain their reward. Meditate on concentration as Brahman."

"Sir, is there anything higher than concentration?"

"Yes, insight is higher than concentration. Through insight we understand all branches of learning, and we understand what is right and what is wrong, what is true and what is false, what is good and what is bad, what is pleasant and what is unpleasant. This world and the other worlds we understand through insight. Meditate on insight as Brahman."

In like manner Sanatkumara taught Narada to meditate on Brahman as power, as food, as water, as fire, as ether, and to meditate on him as memory, as hope, and as the principle of life.

Then said Sanatkumara: "But, verily, he is the true knower who knows eternal Truth."

"Revered sir, I wish to be a true knower."

"Then ask to know of that infinite Reality."

"Sir, I wish to know of it."

"It is only when a man has realized eternal Truth that he declares it. He who reflects upon it realizes it. Without reflection it is not realized.

"And only he who has faith and reverence reflects on eternal Truth.

"And only he who attends on a Guru gains faith and reverence.

"And only he attends on a Guru who struggles to achieve self-control.

"And only he achieves self-control who finds joy in it. Ask to know of this joy."

"Sir, I wish to know of it."

"The Infinite is the source of joy. There is no joy in the finite. Only in the Infinite is there joy. Ask to know of the Infinite."

"Sir, I wish to know of it."

"Where one sees nothing but the One, hears nothing but the One, knows nothing but the One —there is the Infinite. Where one sees another, hears another, knows another—there is the finite. The Infinite is immortal, the finite is mortal."

"In what does the Infinite rest?"

"In its own glory—nay, not even in that. In

the world it is said that cows and horses, elephants and gold, slaves, wives, fields, and houses are man's glory—but these are poor and finite things. How shall the Infinite rest anywhere but in itself?"

"The Infinite is below, above, behind, before, to the right, to the left. I am all this. This Infinite is the Self. The Self is below, above, behind, before, to the right, to the left. I am all this. One who knows, meditates upon, and realizes the truth of the Self—such an one delights in the Self, revels in the Self, rejoices in the Self. He becomes master of himself, and master of all the worlds. Slaves are they who know not this truth.

"He who knows, meditates upon, and realizes this truth of the Self, finds that everything—primal energy, ether, fire, water, and all other elements, mind, will, concentration, speech, sacred hymns and scriptures, indeed the whole universe—issues forth from it.

"It is written: *He who has realized eternal Truth does not see death, nor illness, nor pain; he sees everything as the Self, and obtains all.*

"The Self is one, and it has become all things.

"When the senses are purified, the heart is purified; when the heart is purified, there is constant and unceasing remembrance of the Self; when there is constant and unceasing remembrance of the

Self, all bonds are loosed and freedom is attained."

Thus the venerable Sanatkumara taught Narada, who was pure in heart, how to pass from darkness into light.

Within the city of Brahman, which is the body, there is the heart, and within the heart there is a little house. This house has the shape of a lotus, and within it dwells that which is to be sought after, inquired about, and realized.

What then is that which, dwelling within this little house, this lotus of the heart, is to be sought after, inquired about, and realized?

As large as the universe outside, even so large is the universe within the lotus of the heart. Within it are heaven and earth, the sun, the moon, the lightning, and all the stars. What is in the macrocosm is in this microcosm.

All things that exist, all beings and all desires, are in the city of Brahman; what then becomes of them when old age approaches and the body dissolves in death?

Though old age comes to the body, the lotus of the heart does not grow old. At death of the body, it does not die. The lotus of the heart, where Brahman exists in all his glory—that, and not the body, is the true city of Brahman. Brahman, dwelling therein, is untouched by any deed, ageless, deathless, free from grief, free from hunger and from thirst. His desires are right desires, and his desires are fulfilled.

As here on earth all the wealth that one earns is but transitory, so likewise transitory are the heavenly enjoyments acquired by the performance of sacrifices. Therefore those who die without having realized the Self and its right desires find no permanent happiness in any world to which they go; while those who have realized the Self and its right desires find permanent happiness everywhere.

If the sage desires to see his fathers of the spirit-world, lo, his fathers come to meet him. In their company he is happy.

And if he desires to see his mothers of the spirit-world, lo, his mothers come to meet him. In their company he is happy.

And if he desires to see his brothers of the spirit-world, lo, his brothers come to meet him. In their company he is happy.

And if he desires to see his sisters of the spirit-world, lo, his sisters come to meet him. In their company he is happy.

And if he desires to see his friends of the spirit-world, lo, his friends come to meet him. In their company he is happy.

And if he desires heavenly perfumes and garlands, lo, heavenly perfumes and garlands come
to him. In their possession he is happy.

And if he desires heavenly food and drink, lo,
heavenly food and drink come to him. In their
possession he is happy.

And if he desires heavenly song and music, lo,
heavenly song and music come to him. In their
possession he is happy.

Indeed, whatsoever such a knower of Brahman
may desire, straightway it is his; and having obtained it, he is exalted of men. The fulfillment of
right desires is within reach of everyone, but a veil
of illusion obstructs the ignorant. That is why,
though they desire to see their dead, their beloved,
they cannot see them.

Do we wish for our beloved, among the living
or among the dead, or is there aught else for which
we long, yet, for all our longing, do not obtain?—
lo, all shall be ours if we but dive deep within,
even to the lotus of the heart, where dwells the
Lord. Yea, the object of every right desire is within
our reach, though unseen, concealed by a veil of
illusion.

As one not knowing that a golden treasure lies
buried beneath his feet, may walk over it again
and again, yet never find it, so all beings live every
moment in the city of Brahman, yet never find

him, because of the veil of illusion by which he is concealed.

The Self resides within the lotus of the heart. Knowing this, consecrated to the Self, the sage enters daily that holy sanctuary.

Absorbed in the Self, the sage is freed from identity with the body and lives in blissful consciousness. The Self is the immortal, the fearless; the Self is Brahman. This Brahman is eternal Truth.

The Self within the heart is like a boundary which divides the world from THAT. Day and night cross not that boundary, nor old age, nor death; neither grief nor pleasure, neither good nor evil deeds. All evil shuns THAT. For THAT is free from impurity: by impurity can it never be touched.

Wherefore he who has crossed that boundary, and has realized the Self, if he is blind, ceases to be blind; if he is wounded, ceases to be wounded; if he is afflicted, ceases to be afflicted. When that boundary is crossed, night becomes day; for the world of Brahman is light itself.

And that world of Brahman is reached by those who practice continence. For the knower of eternal truth knows it through continence. And what is known as worship, that also is continence.

For a man worships the Lord by continence, and thus attains him.

What people call salvation is really continence. For through continence man is freed from ignorance. And what is known as the vow of silence, that too is really continence. For a man through continence realizes the Self and lives in quiet contemplation.

What people call dwelling in the forest, that is really continence.

In the world of Brahman there is a lake whose waters are like nectar, and whosoever tastes thereof is straightway drunk with joy; and beside that lake is a tree which yields the juice of immortality. Into this world they cannot enter who do not practice continence.

For the world of Brahman belongs to those who practice continence. They alone enter that world and drink from that lake of nectar. For them there is freedom in all the worlds.

It was said of old:

The Self, which is free from impurities, from old age and death, from grief, from hunger and thirst, which desires nothing but what it ought to desire, and resolves nothing but what it ought to resolve, is to be sought after, is to be inquired

*about, is to be realized. He who learns about the
Self and realizes it obtains all the worlds and all
desires.*

The gods and demons both heard of this truth,
and they thought to themselves, "Let us seek after
and realize this Self, so that we may obtain all the
worlds and all desires."

Thereupon Indra from the gods, and Virochana
from the demons, went to Prajapati, the renowned
teacher. For thirty-two years they lived with him
as pupils. Then Prajapati asked them why they
had both lived with him so long.

"We have heard," they replied, "that one who
realizes the Self obtains all the worlds and all desires. We have lived here because we want to learn
of this Self."

Then said Prajapati: "That which is seen in
the eye—that is the Self. That is immortal, that
is fearless, and that is Brahman."

"Sir," inquired the disciples, "is that the Self
which is seen reflected in the water, or in a mirror?"

"The Self is indeed seen reflected in these," was
the reply. Then Prajapati added, "Look at yourselves in the water, and whatever you do not understand, come and tell me about it."

Indra and Virochana gazed on their reflections

in the water, and returning to the sage, they said: "Sir, we have seen the Self; we have seen even the hair and the nails."

Then Prajapati bade them don their finest clothes and look again in the water. This they did, and returning to the sage, they said: "We have seen the Self, exactly like ourselves, well adorned and in our finest clothes."

To which Prajapati rejoined: "The Self is indeed seen in these. The Self is immortal and fearless, and it is Brahman." And the pupils went away well pleased.

But Prajapati, looking after them, lamented thus: "Both of them departed without analyzing or discriminating, and without truly comprehending the Self. Whosoever follows a false doctrine of the Self will perish."

Now Virochana, satisfied for his part that he had found out the Self, returned to the demons and began to teach them that the body alone is to be worshiped, that the body alone is to be served, and that he who worships the body and serves the body gains both worlds, this and the next. Such doctrine is, in very truth, the doctrine of the demons!

But Indra, on his way back to the gods, realized the uselessness of this knowledge. "As this

Self," he reasoned, "seems to be well adorned when the body is well adorned, well dressed when the body is well dressed, so will it be blind when the body is blind, lame when the body is lame, deformed when the body is deformed. When the body dies, this same Self will also die! In such knowledge I can see no good."

So he returned to Prajapati and asked for further instruction. Prajapati required him to live with him for another thirty-two years, after which time he taught him thus:

"That which moves about in dreams, enjoying sensuous delights and clothed in glory, that is the Self. That is immortal, that is fearless, and that is Brahman."

Pleased with what he had heard, Indra again departed. But before he had reached the other gods he realized the uselessness of this knowledge also. "True it is," he thought to himself, "that this Self is not blind when the body is blind, nor lame or hurt when the body is lame or hurt. But even in dreams it is conscious of many sufferings. So in this doctrine also I can see no good."

So he went back to Prajapati for further instruction. Prajapati now bade him live with him for another thirty-two years, and when the time had passed taught him, saying, "When a man

is sound asleep, free from dreams, and at perfect
rest—that is the Self. The Self is immortal and
fearless, and it is Brahman."

Indra went away. But before he had reached his
home, he felt the uselessness even of this knowledge. "In reality," thought he, "one does not know
oneself as this or as that while asleep. One is not
conscious, in fact, of any existence at all. The
state of one in deep sleep is next to annihilation. I
can see no good in this knowledge either."

So once more Indra went back to Prajapati,
who bade him stay with him yet five years, and
when the time had passed, made known to him
the highest truth of the Self, saying:

"This body is mortal, always gripped by death,
but within it dwells the immortal Self. This Self,
when associated in our consciousness with the
body, is subject to pleasure and pain; and so long
as this association continues, freedom from pleasure and pain can no man find. But as this association ceases, there cease also the pleasure and the
pain.

"Rising above physical consciousness, knowing
the Self to be distinct from the senses and the mind
—knowing it in its true light—one rejoices and
is free."

The gods, the luminous ones, meditate on the

Self, and by so doing obtain all the worlds and all desires. In like manner, whosoever among mortals knows the Self, meditates upon it, and realizes it—he too obtains all the worlds and all desires.

X

BRIHADARANYAKA

THE Self is the dearest of all things, and only through the Self is anything else dear. The Self is the origin of all finite happiness, but it is itself pure bliss, transcending definition. It remains unaffected by deeds, good or bad. It is beyond feeling and beyond knowledge, but it is not beyond the meditation of the sage.

BRIHADARANYAKA

OM . . .
Filled   with Brahman are the things we see,
Filled   with Brahman are the things we see not,
From out of Brahman floweth all that is:
From Brahman all—yet is he still the same.
OM . . . Peace—peace—peace.

Lead me from the unreal to the real.
Lead me from darkness to light.
Lead me from death to immortality.

THE WORLD EXISTED first as seed, which as it grew and developed took on names and forms. As a razor in its case or as fire in wood, so dwells the Self, the Lord of the universe, in all forms, even to the tips of the fingers. Yet the ignorant do not know him, for behind the names and forms he remains hidden. When one breathes, one knows him as breath; when one speaks, one knows him as speech; when one sees, one knows him as the eye; when one hears, one knows him as the ear; when one thinks, one knows him as the mind. All these are but names related to his acts; and he who worships the Self as one or another of them does not know him, for of them he is neither one nor another. Wherefore let a man worship him as the Self, and as the Self alone. The perfection which is the Self is the goal of all beings. For by knowing the Self one knows all. He who knows the Self is honored of all men and attains to blessedness.

This Self, which is nearer to us than anything else, is indeed dearer than a son, dearer than wealth, dearer than all beside. Let a man worship the Self alone as dear, for if he worship the Self alone as dear, the object of his love will never perish.

This universe, before it was created, existed as Brahman. "I am Brahman": thus did Brahman know himself. Knowing himself, he became the Self of all beings. Among the gods, he who awakened to the knowledge of the Self became Brahman; and the same was true among the seers. The seer Vamadeva, realizing Brahman, knew that he himself was the Self of mankind as well as of the sun. Therefore, now also, whoever realizes Brahman knows that he himself is the Self in all creatures. Even the gods cannot harm such a man, since he becomes their innermost Self.

Now if a man worship Brahman, thinking Brahman is one and he another, he has not the true knowledge.

This universe, before it was created, existed as Brahman. Brahman created out of himself priests, warriors, tradesmen, and servants, among both gods and men.

Then he created the most excellent Law. There is nothing higher than the Law. The Law is the truth. Therefore it is said that if a man speak the truth he declares the Law, and if he declare the Law he speaks the truth. The Law and the truth are one.

Now if a man depart this life without knowing the kingdom of the Self, he, because of that ignorance, does not enjoy the bliss of liberation. He dies without reaching his goal. Nay, even if a man ignorant of the kingdom of the Self should do virtuous deeds on earth, he would not arrive through them at everlasting life; for the effects of his deeds would finally be exhausted. Wherefore let him know the kingdom of the Self, and that alone. The virtue of him who meditates on the kingdom of the Self is never exhausted: for the Self is the source from which all virtue springs.

The Self, out of which the sun rises, and into which it sets—that alone do the wise make their goal.

Gargya, son of Valaka, was a good talker, but exceedingly vain. Coming one day into the pres-

ence of Ajatasatru, king of Benares, he accosted
him with boastful speech.

Gargya

I will teach you of Brahman.

Ajatasatru

Indeed? Well, just for that kind proposal you
should be rewarded with a thousand cows. People nowadays flock to King Janaka to speak and
hear of Brahman; I am pleased that you have come
to me instead.

Gargya

He who is the being in the sun and at the same
time the being in the eye; he who, having entered
the body through the eye, resides in the heart of
man and is the doer and the experiencer—him I
meditate upon as Brahman.

Ajatasatru

Nay, nay! Do not speak thus of Brahman. That
being I worship as transcendental, luminous, supreme. He who meditates upon Brahman as such
goes beyond all created beings and becomes the
glorious ruler of all.

Gargya

The being who is in the moon and at the same time in the mind—him I meditate upon as Brahman.

Ajatasatru

Nay, nay! Do not speak thus of Brahman. That being I worship as infinite, clad in purity, blissful, resplendent. He who meditates upon Brahman as such lacks nothing and is forever happy.

Gargya

The being who is in the lightning and at the same time in the heart—him I meditate upon as Brahman.

Ajatasatru

Nay, nay! Do not speak thus of Brahman. That being I worship as power. He who meditates upon Brahman as such becomes powerful, and his children after him.

Gargya

The being who is in the sky and at the same time in the heart—him I meditate upon as Brahman.

Ajatasatru

Nay, nay! Do not speak thus of Brahman. That being I worship as all-pervading, changeless. He who meditates upon Brahman as such is blessed with children and with cattle. The thread of his progeny shall never be cut.

Gargya

The being who is in the wind and who at the same time is the breath within—him I meditate upon as Brahman.

Ajatasatru

Nay, nay! Do not speak thus of Brahman. That being I worship as the Lord, invincible and unconquerable. He who meditates upon Brahman as such becomes himself invincible and unconquerable.

Gargya

The being who is in the fire and at the same time in the heart—him I meditate upon as Brahman.

Ajatasatru

Nay, nay! Do not speak thus of Brahman. That being I worship as forgiving. He who meditates

upon Brahman as such becomes himself forgiving,
and his children after him.

Gargya

The being who is in the water and at the same
time in the heart—him I meditate upon as Brahman.

Ajatasatru

Nay, nay! Do not speak thus of Brahman. That
being I worship as harmony. He who meditates
upon Brahman as such knows only what is har-
monious. Of him are born tranquil children.

Gargya

The being who is in the mirror—him I meditate upon as Brahman.

Ajatasatru

Nay, nay! Do not speak thus of Brahman. That
being I worship as effulgent. He who meditates
upon Brahman as such becomes himself effulgent,
and his children after him. He shines brighter
than all who approach him.

Gargya

The sound that follows a man as he walks—
that I meditate upon as Brahman.

Ajatasatru

Nay, nay! Do not speak thus of Brahman. That being I worship as the vital force. He who meditates upon Brahman as such reaches his full age in this world; breath does not leave him before his time.

Gargya

The being who pervades space—him I meditate upon as Brahman.

Ajatasatru

Nay, nay! Do not speak thus of Brahman. That being I worship as a second self, which can never be separated from me. He who meditates upon Brahman as such is never lonely, and his followers never forsake him.

Gargya

The being who dwells in the heart as intelligence—him I meditate upon as Brahman.

Ajatasatru

Nay, nay! Do not speak thus of Brahman. That being I worship as the lord of will. He who meditates upon Brahman as such achieves self-control, and his children after him.

Gargya ceased speaking. Ajatasatru, continuing, questioned him.

Ajatasatru

Is that all that you know of Brahman?

Gargya (*humbly*)

That is all that I know.

Ajatasatru

By knowing only so much, one cannot profess to know Brahman.

Gargya (*humbly*)

Please, sir, accept me as a disciple, and teach me of Brahman.

Ajatasatru

It is unnatural that a Brahmin should approach a Kshatriya and a king to learn of Brahman. However, I will teach you.

So saying, Ajatasatru took Gargya by the hand and rose. Then, as the two walked side by side, they came to a sleeping man.

Ajatasatru (*to the sleeper*)

O thou great one, clad in white raiment, O Soma, O king!

At first the man did not stir. Then, as Ajatas-
atru touched him, he awoke.

Ajatasatru (to Gargya)

This man, who is a conscious, intelligent being
—where was he when he was thus asleep, and how
did he thus wake up? (*Gargya was silent.*) When
this man, who is a conscious, intelligent being, is
thus in deep sleep, he enters into the Self, within
the lotus of the heart, having withdrawn into
himself both his senses and his mind. When his
senses and his mind are thus withdrawn, he is said
to be absorbed in the Self.

In this state he knows nothing; he enters into
the seventy-two thousand nerves which go out
from the lotus of the heart. Even as a young man,
or an emperor, or the best of Brahmins, when
he has experienced the ecstasy of love straightway
takes sweet repose, so does a man deep in sleep
find rest.

But when he sleeps, but also dreams, he lives
in a world of his own. He may dream that he is
a king, or that he is the best of Brahmins; he may
dream that he is an angel, or that he is a beast. As
an emperor, having obtained the objects of enjoyment, moves about at will in his dominions, so
the sleeper, gathering up the impressions of sense,

compounds them into dreams according to his desires.

As threads come out of the spider, as little sparks come out of the fire, so all the senses, all the worlds, all the gods, yea, all beings, issue forth from the Self. His secret name is Truth of the Truth.

———————

Yagnavalkya (to his wife)

Maitreyi, I am resolved to renounce the world and begin the life of renunciation. I wish therefore to divide my property between you and my other wife, Katyayani.

Maitreyi

My lord, if this whole earth belonged to me, with all its wealth, should I through its possession attain immortality?

Yagnavalkya

No. Your life would be like that of the rich. None can possibly hope to attain immortality through wealth.

Maitreyi

Then what need have I of wealth? Please, my lord, tell me what you know about the way to immortality.

Yagnavalkya

Dear to me have you always been, Maitreyi, and
now you ask to learn of that truth which is nearest my heart. Come, sit by me. I will explain it to
you. Meditate on what I say.

It is not for the sake of the husband, my beloved, that the husband is dear, but for the sake
of the Self.

It is not for the sake of the wife, my beloved,
that the wife is dear, but for the sake of the Self.

It is not for the sake of the children, my beloved, that the children are dear, but for the sake
of the Self.

It is not for the sake of wealth, my beloved,
that wealth is dear, but for the sake of the Self.

It is not for the sake of the Brahmins, my beloved, that the Brahmins are held in reverence, but
for the sake of the Self.

It is not for the sake of the Kshatriyas, my beloved, that the Kshatriyas are held in honor, but
for the sake of the Self.

It is not for the sake of the higher worlds, my
beloved, that the higher worlds are desired, but for
the sake of the Self.

It is not for the sake of the gods, my beloved,
that the gods are worshiped, but for the sake of
the Self.

It is not for the sake of the creatures, my beloved, that the creatures are dear, but for the sake of the Self.

It is not for the sake of itself, my beloved, that anything whatever is esteemed, but for the sake of the Self.

The Self, beloved Maitreyi, is to be known. Hear about it, reflect upon it, meditate upon it. By knowing the Self, my beloved, through hearing, reflection, and meditation, one comes to know all things.

Let the Brahmin ignore him who thinks that the Brahmin is different from the Self.

Let the Kshatriya ignore him who thinks that the Kshatriya is different from the Self.

Let the higher worlds ignore him who thinks that the higher worlds are different from the Self.

Let the gods ignore him who thinks that the gods are different from the Self.

Let all creatures ignore him who thinks that the creatures are different from the Self.

Let all ignore him who thinks that anything whatever is different from the Self.

The priest, the warrior, the higher worlds, the gods, the creatures, whatsoever things there be— these are the Self

As, when the drum is beaten, its various particular notes are not heard apart from the whole,

but in the total sound all its notes are heard; as,
when the conch-shell is blown, its various particular notes are not heard apart from the whole, but
in the total sound all its notes are heard; as, when
the vina is played, its various particular notes are
not heard apart from the whole, but in the total
sound all its notes are heard—so, through the
knowledge of the Self, Pure Intelligence, all things
and beings are known. There is no existence apart
from the Self.

As smoke and sparks arise from a lighted fire
kindled with damp fuel, even so, Maitreyi, have
been breathed forth from the Eternal all knowledge and all wisdom—what we know as the Rig
Veda, the Yajur Veda, and the rest. They are the
breath of the Eternal.

As for water the one center is the ocean, as for
touch the one center is the skin, as for smell the one
center is the nose, as for taste the one center is the
tongue, as for form the one center is the eyes, as
for sound the one center is the ears, as for thought
the one center is the mind, as for divine wisdom
the one center is the heart—so for all beings the
one center is the Self.

As a lump of salt when thrown into water melts
away and the lump cannot be taken out, but wherever we taste the water it is salty, even so, O
Maitreyi, the individual self, dissolved, is the

Eternal—pure consciousness, infinite and transcendent. Individuality arises by identification of the Self, through ignorance, with the elements; and with the disappearance of consciousness of the many, in divine illumination, it disappears. Where there is consciousness of the Self, individuality is no more.

This it is, O my beloved, that I wanted to tell you.

Maitreyi

"Where there is consciousness of the Self, individuality is no more": this that you say, my lord, confuses me.

Yagnavalkya

My beloved, let nothing I have said confuse you. But meditate well the truth that I have spoken.

As long as there is duality, one sees *the other*, one hears *the other*, one smells *the other*, one speaks to *the other*, one thinks of *the other*, one knows *the other*; but when for the illumined soul the all is dissolved in the Self, who is there to be seen by whom, who is there to be smelt by whom, who is there to be heard by whom, who is there to be spoken to by whom, who is there to be thought of by whom, who is there to be known by whom?

Ah, Maitreyi, my beloved, the Intelligence which reveals all—by what shall it be revealed? By whom shall the Knower be known? The Self is described as *not this, not that*. It is incomprehensible, for it cannot be comprehended; undecaying, for it never decays; unattached, for it never attaches itself; unbound, for it is never bound. By whom, O my beloved, shall the Knower be known?

This it is that I teach you, O Maitreyi. This is the truth of immortality.

So saying, Yagnavalkya entered upon the path of renunciation.

This earth is honey for all beings, and all beings are honey for this earth. The intelligent, immortal being, the soul of this earth, and the intelligent, immortal being, the soul in the individual being—each is honey to the other. Brahman is the soul in each; he indeed is the Self in all. He is all.

This water is honey for all beings, and all beings are honey for this water. The intelligent, immortal being, the soul of this water, and the intelligent, immortal being, the soul in the individual being—each is honey to the other. Brahman is the soul in each; he indeed is the Self in all. He is all.

This fire is honey for all beings, and all beings

are honey for this fire. The intelligent, immortal
being, the soul of this fire, and the intelligent, immortal being, the soul in the individual being—
each is honey to the other. Brahman is the soul in
each; he indeed is the Self in all. He is all.

This air is honey for all beings, and all beings
are honey for this air. The intelligent, immortal
being, the soul of this air, and the intelligent, immortal being, the soul in the individual being—
each is honey to the other. Brahman is the soul in
each; he indeed is the Self in all. He is all.

This sun is honey for all beings, and all beings
are honey for this sun. The intelligent, immortal
being, the soul of this sun, and the intelligent,
immortal being, the soul in the individual being—
each is honey to the other. Brahman is the soul
in each; he indeed is the Self in all. He is all.

This space is honey for all beings, and all beings
are honey for this space. The intelligent, immortal
being, the soul of this space, and the intelligent,
immortal being, the soul in the individual being—
each is honey to the other. Brahman is the soul in
each; he indeed is the Self in all. He is all.

This moon is honey for all beings, and all beings are honey for this moon. The intelligent, immortal being, the soul of this moon and the intelligent, immortal being, the soul in the individual
being—each is honey to the other. Brahman is the

soul in each; he indeed is the Self in all. He is all.

This lightning is honey for all beings, and all beings are honey for this lightning. The intelligent, immortal being, the soul of this lightning, and the intelligent, immortal being, the soul in the individual being—each is honey to the other. Brahman is the soul in each; he indeed is the Self in all. He is all.

This thunder is honey for all beings, and all beings are honey for this thunder. The intelligent, immortal being, the soul of this thunder, and the intelligent, immortal being, the soul in the individual being—each is honey to the other. Brahman is the soul in each; he indeed is the Self in all. He is all.

This ether is honey for all beings, and all beings are honey for this ether. The intelligent, immortal being, the soul of this ether, and the intelligent, immortal being, the soul in the individual being—each is honey to the other. Brahman is the soul in each; he indeed is the Self in all. He is all.

This law is honey for all beings, and all beings are honey for this law. The intelligent, immortal being, the soul of this law, and the intelligent, immortal being, the soul in the individual being—each is honey to the other. Brahman is the soul in each; he indeed is the Self in all. He is all.

This truth is honey for all beings, and all beings

are honey for this truth. The intelligent, immortal
being, the soul of this truth, and the intelligent,
immortal being, the soul in the individual being—
each is honey to the other. Brahman is the soul in
each; he indeed is the Self in all. He is all.

This race of men is honey for all beings, and all
beings are honey for this race of men. The intelligent, immortal being, the soul of this race of men,
and the intelligent, immortal being, the soul in the
individual being—each is honey to the other. Brahman is the soul in each; he indeed is the Self in all.
He is all.

This Self is honey for all beings, and all beings
are honey for this Self. The intelligent, immortal
being, the soul of this Self, and the intelligent,
immortal being, the soul in the individual being—
each is honey to the other. Brahman is the soul in
each; he indeed is the Self in all. He is all.

This Self is the lord of all beings, the king of all
beings. As the spokes are held together in the hub
and in the felly of a wheel, just so all beings, all
creatures, all gods, all worlds, all lives, are held
together in the Self.

He made bodies with two feet, he made bodies
with four feet. He entered into all bodies, and
because he dwells within the lotus of the heart,
he is known as *Purusha*. There is nothing that is

not surrounded by him, nothing that is not filled
by him.

He assumed all forms. He assumed all forms to
reveal himself in all forms. He, the Lord, is revealed in all forms through his Maya. He is tens,
and thousands, many and endless.

This Brahman is without cause, without effect,
without inside or outside. This Brahman is the
Self."

Janaka, King of Videha, on a certain occasion
performed a sacrifice and in connection therewith
distributed costly gifts. Among those who attended
the ceremony were the wise men of Kuru and of
Panchala. King Janaka observed them and wanted
to find out which was the wisest.

Now it happened that the king kept a thousand
cows enclosed in a pen, and between the horns of
every one of them were fastened ten gold coins.

"Venerable Brahmins," said King Janaka, "let
him who is the wisest among you take these cows
home."

The Brahmins dared not stir, save Yagnavalkya
alone.

"My learned son," said Yagnavalkya to his
disciple, "drive home my cows."

"Hurrah!" cried the lad, and made after them.

The rest of the Brahmins were enraged. "How dare he call himself the wisest!" they shouted. At last, Aswala, priest to King Janaka, accosted Yagnavalkya, saying:

"Yagnavalkya, are you quite sure you are the wisest among us?"

"I bow down," replied Yagnavalkya, "to the wisest. But I want those cows!"

Then Aswala began to question him.

Aswala

Yagnavalkya, since everything connected with sacrificial rites is pervaded by death, and is subject to death, by what means can the worshiper overcome death?

Yagnavalkya

By the knowledge of the identity between the worshiper, the fire, and the ritual word. For the ritual word is indeed the worshiper, and the ritual word is the fire, and the fire, which is one with Brahman, is the worshiper. This knowledge leads to liberation; this knowledge leads one beyond death.

Aswala held his peace. But Artabhaga asked:

Yagnavalkya, everything is the food of death. Is there any power for which death is food?

Yagnavalkya

Indeed, yes. Fire devours everything, and fire, again, is the food of water. Similarly there is a death to death. The knower of the truth of Brahman overcomes death.

Artabhaga

Yagnavalkya, when such an one gives up his body, do his perceptive faculties, along with his mind, go out of him, or do they not?

Yagnavalkya

They do not. They merge in the final cause, the Self. The body lies lifeless, inflated, and swollen.

Artabhaga held his peace. Then Ushasta asked:

Yagnavalkya, what is the ultimate, the immediate Brahman, Brahman himself alone, directly realized as such, the Self which dwells within all?

Yagnavalkya (*pointing to his heart*)

This, thy Self, which is within all.

Ushasta

Which self, O Yagnavalkya, is within all?

Yagnavalkya

That which breathes in is thy Self, which is within all. That which breathes down is thy Self, which is within all. That which diffuses breath is thy Self, which is within all. That which breathes out is thy Self, which is within all. Again I reply: This, thy Self, which is within all.

Ushasta

As one might say, in distinguishing a cow from a horse, that the cow is the animal that walks, and the horse is the animal that runs, exactly so simple, so clear, O wise one, has been your teaching about Brahman! But tell me, I ask again, who is the ultimate, the immediate Brahman, Brahman himself alone, directly realized as such, the Self which dwells within all?

Yagnavalkya

This, thy Self, which is within all.

Ushasta

Which self, O Yagnvalkya, is within all?

Yagnavalkya

Thou canst not see the seer of the sight, thou canst not hear the hearer of the sound, thou canst not think the thinker of the thought, thou canst not know the knower of the known. Again I reply: This, thy Self, which is within all. Anything that is not the Self perishes.

Ushasta held his peace. Kahola asked:

Yagnavalkya, what is the ultimate, the immediate Brahman, Brahman himself alone, directly realized as such, the Self which dwells within all?

Yagnavalkya

This, thy Self, which is within all.

Kahola

Which self, O Yagnavalkya, is within all?

Yagnavalkya

That which is beyond hunger, thirst, grief, delusion, decay, and death. Having realized this Self, the sages renounce the craving for progeny, wealth, and existence in the other worlds, and live the life of mendicants. The craving for progeny leads to the craving for wealth, and the craving for wealth

to the craving for existence in the other worlds.
Thus there are two cravings—craving for a life of
enjoyment here, and craving for a life of greater
enjoyment hereafter. Therefore should a sage,
when he has fully attained the knowledge of the
Self, desire to live with that knowledge as his
only refuge. When he has fully attained the
knowledge of the Self, and realized it as his only
refuge, he should devote himself exclusively to
contemplation of the Self. He alone is the true
knower of Brahman who directs his mind towards
the Self, and shuns all other thoughts as distrac-
tions. How does such a knower of Brahman act
and conduct himself? Whatever he may do or
howsoever he may conduct himself, he is free from
craving, and is forever established in the knowledge of Brahman. Anything that is not the Self
perishes.

Kahola held his peace. Uddalaka asked:

Yagnavalkya, we live as students in Madra, in
the house of Kapya. His wife was once possessed
by a Gandharva, a celestial singer. We asked the
Gandharva who he was. He replied that he was
Kabandha, and proceeded to question Kapya thus:
"Dost thou know that thread whereon this life,
the next life, and all beings are strung together?"
Kapya did not know. The Gandharva continued:

"Dost thou know that Inner Ruler who controls, from within, this life, the next life, and all beings?" Kapya did not know. The Gandharva then said: "He who knows that thread and that Inner Ruler knows Brahman, knows the worlds, knows the gods, knows the Vedas, knows the creatures, knows the Self—knows all things." I myself know these things that the Gandharva taught. Yagnavalkya, if thou, without knowing that thread and that Inner Ruler, take the cows that belong only to the wisest, accursed shalt thou be.

Yagnavalkya

I know that thread and that Inner Ruler.

Uddalaka

Anybody can say, "I know, I know." Tell us what you know.

Yagnavalkya

The subtle principle of life is that thread whereon this life and the next life and all beings are strung. Hence, when a man dies, they say his limbs are loosed, for while he lives they are held together by that principle of life.

Uddalaka

That is true, Yagnavalkya. Now speak of the Inner Ruler.

Yagnavalkya

He who dwells on earth, but is separate from
the earth, whom the earth does not know, whose
body the earth is, and who controls the earth from
within—he, the Self, is the Inner Ruler, the Immortal.

He who dwells in water but is separate from
water, whom water does not know, whose body
water is, and who controls water from within—
he, the Self, is the Inner Ruler, the Immortal.

He who dwells in fire but is separate from fire,
whom fire does not know, whose body fire is, and
who controls fire from within—he, the Self, is the
Inner Ruler, the Immortal.

He who dwells in the sky, in the air, in heaven,
in the four quarters, in the sun, in the moon, in
the stars, in ether, in darkness, in light, but is
separate from them, whom none of them knows,
whose body they are, and who controls them from
within—he, the Self, is the Inner Ruler, the Immortal.

He who dwells in all beings but is separate
from all beings, whom no being knows, whose
body all beings are, and who controls all beings
from within—he, the Self, is the Inner Ruler, the
Immortal.

He who dwells in odor, speech, sight, hearing,

and touch, but is separate from them; whom odor, speech, sight, hearing, and touch do not know; whose body is odor, speech, sight, hearing, and touch; and who controls them all from within— he, the Self, is the Inner Ruler, the Immortal.

He who dwells in the mind, but is separate from the mind, whom the mind does not know, whose body the mind is, and who controls the mind from within—he, the Self, is the Inner Ruler, the Immortal.

He who dwells in the intellect, but is separate from the intellect, whom the intellect does not know, whose body is the intellect, and who controls the intellect from within—he, the Self, is the Inner Ruler, the Immortal.

Unseen, but the seer; unheard, but the hearer; unthinkable, but the thinker; unknown, but the knower—there is no other seer but he, there is no other hearer but he, there is no other thinker but he, there is no other knower but he. He, the Self, is the Inner Ruler, the Immortal.

Anything that is not the Self perishes.

Uddalaka held his peace. Then arose Gargi, the daughter of Vachaknu, and addressed the sages:

Revered Brahmins, I shall ask Yagnavalkya two questions. If he is able to answer them, no one

among you can ever defeat him. He will be the great
expounder of the truth of Brahman.

Yagnavalkya

Ask, O Gargi.

Gargi

Yagnavalkya, as the son of a warrior from Kasi
or Videha might string his loosened bow and with
two deadly arrows in his hand rise to give battle,
even so have I risen to fight thee with two questions. Answer my questions.

Yagnavalkya

Ask, O Gargi.

Gargi

Yagnavalkya, that of which they say that it is
above heaven and below the earth, which is between heaven and earth as well, and which was, is,
and shall be—tell me in what it is woven, warp
and woof?

Yagnavalkya

That of which they say, O Gargi, that it is
above heaven and below the earth, which is between heaven and earth as well, and which was, is,

and shall be—that is woven, warp and woof, in the ether.

Gargi

Thou hast answered my first question. I bow to thee, O Yagnavalkya. Be ready now to answer my second question.

Yagnavalkya

Ask, O Gargi.

Gargi

In what is that ether woven, warp and woof?

Yagnavalkya

The seers, O Gargi, call that Akshara—the changeless Reality. He is neither gross nor fine, neither short nor long, neither hot nor cold, neither light nor dark, neither of the nature of air, nor of the nature of ether. He is without relations. He is without taste or smell, without eyes, ears, speech, mind, vigor, breath, mouth; he is without measure; he is without inside or outside. He enjoys nothing; nothing enjoys him.

At the command of that Akshara, O Gargi, sun and moon hold their course. At the command of that Akshara, O Gargi, heaven and earth keep their position. At the command of that Akshara,

O Gargi, moments, hours, days and nights, fort-
nights and months, seasons and years—all follow
their path. At the command of that Akshara, O
Gargi, rivers, issuing from the snowy mountains,
flow on, some eastward, some westward, others in
other directions.

He, O Gargi, who in this world, without knowing this Akshara, offers oblations, performs sacrifices, practices austerities, even though for many
thousands of years, gains little: his offerings and
practices are perishable. He, O Gargi, who departs
this world without knowing the Imperishable, is
pitiable. But he, O Gargi, who departs this world
knowing the Akshara, is wise.

This Akshara, O Gargi, is unseen but is the
seer, is unheard but is the hearer, is unthinkable
but is the thinker, is unknown but is the knower.
There is no seer but he, there is no hearer but he,
there is no thinker but he, there is no knower but
he. In Akshara, verily, O Gargi, the ether is
woven, warp and woof.

Gargi

Revered Brahmins, well may you feel blest if
you get off with bowing before him! No one will
defeat Yagnavalkya, expounder of the truth of
Brahman.

*Gargi held her peace. Yagnavalkya addressed the
sages:*

Revered Brahmins, ask me questions, if you will
—any one of you in the assembly, or all of you.
Or if any one of you so desires, I will question
him. Or I will question all of you.
But the Brahmins held their peace.

OM . . .
On a certain occasion, Janaka, king of Videha,
having seated himself to give audience, saw the
sage Yagnavalkya among his visitors and accosted
him.

Janaka

Yagnavalkya, what brings you here? Do you
come for cattle, or for philosophy?

Yagnavalkya

For both, Your Majesty. I wish to hear what
your teachers may have taught you.

Janaka

Jitwa taught me that the word is Brahman.

Yagnavalkya

As one who from childhood has been instructed

adequately, first by his mother, then by his father, and after that has been initiated into the sacred mysteries by a sage—as such an one should teach, so has Jitwa taught you the truth when he said that the word is Brahman. For what could a person achieve without the word? But did he tell you about the abode and support of this Word-Brahman?

Janaka

No, he did not.

Yagnavalkya

Then you have been only partly taught.

Janaka

Do you, then, teach me, O Yagnavalkya.

Yagnavalkya

The organ of speech is its abode, and ether, the primal cause of the universe, is its eternal support. Meditate upon the word as identical with knowledge.

Janaka

What is knowledge, Yagnavalkya?

Yagnavalkya

The word is knowledge, Your Majesty. For through the word a friend is known, and likewise all knowledge, spiritual or otherwise. Through the word is gained knowledge of this world and of the next. Through the word is obtained knowledge of all creatures. The word, Your Majesty, is the Supreme Brahman.

Janaka

I give you a thousand cows with a bull as big as an elephant for teaching me.

Yagnavalkya

My father was of the opinion that one should not accept any reward from a disciple without fully instructing him. I wish to know what anyone else may have taught you.

Janaka

Udanka taught me that primal energy is Brahman. He did not tell me about its abode and support.

Yagnavalkya

Breath is its abode and ether its support. It should be meditated upon as dear. For life is in-

deed dear. The primal energy is Brahman. Tell me
what more you have been taught.

Janaka

Barku taught me that sight is Brahman. But
he did not teach me its abode and support.

Yagnavalkya

The eye is its abode and ether its support. It
should be meditated upon as truth. For it is by
sight that objects are known. Sight is Brahman.
What more have you learned?

Janaka

Gardabhivipati taught me that hearing is Brahman.

Yagnavalkya

The ear is its abode and ether its support. It
should be meditated upon as limitless. For sound is
carried by space, and space is limitless. Hearing is
Brahman.

Janaka

Satyakama taught me that the mind is Brahman.

Yagnavalkya

The mind is its abode and ether its support. It should be meditated upon as happiness. For by the mind alone is happiness experienced. Mind is Brahman.

Janaka

Vidagdha taught me that the heart is Brahman.

Yagnavalkya

The heart is its abode and ether its support. It should be meditated upon as the resting-place. For all beings find rest in the heart. The heart is Brahman.

Janaka (descending from his throne and humbly addressing the sage)

I bow down to you. Yagnavalkya, please teach me.

Yagnavalkya

Your Majesty, as a person wishing to make a long journey furnishes himself with a chariot or a boat, so have you equipped your mind with sacred wisdom. You are honorable and wealthy, and you have studied the Vedas and learned the Upanishads. Whither then shall you go when you leave this body?

Janaka

I do not know, revered sir.

Yagnavalkya

I will tell you where you will go.

Janaka

Tell me, please.

Yagnavalkya

Indha is the Self identified with the physical self. Viraj, the physical world, is his wife, the object of his enjoyment. The space within the heart is their place of union in dream, when the Self is identified with the subtle body, or mind. The Self in dreamless sleep is identified with the vital force. Beyond this is the Supreme Self—he that has been described as *not this, not that*. He is incomprehensible, for he cannot be comprehended; he is undecaying, for he never decays; he is unattached, for he does not attach himself; he is unfettered, for nothing can fetter him. He is never hurt. You have attained him who is free from fear, O Janaka, and free from birth and death.

Janaka

May that fearlessness come to you who teach us

fearlessness. I bow down to you. Behold this empire of Videha, as well as I myself, at your service.

Once when Yagnavalkya came to the court of King Janaka, the King welcomed him with a question.

Janaka

Yagnavalkya, what serves as the light for man?

Yagnavalkya

The light of the sun, Your Majesty; for by the light of the sun man sits, goes out, does his work, and returns home.

Janaka

True indeed, Yagnavalkya. But when the sun has set, what serves then as his light?

Yagnavalkya

The moon is then his light.

Janaka

When the sun has set, O Yagnavalkya, and the moon has set, what serves then as his light?

Yagnavalkya

The fire is then his light.

Janaka

When the sun has set, O Yagnavalkya, and the moon has set, and the fire has gone out, what serves then as his light?

Yagnavalkya

Sound is then his light; for with sound alone as his light, man sits, goes out, does his work, and returns home. Even though he cannot see his own hand, yet when he hears a sound he moves towards it.

Janaka

True indeed, O Yagnavalkya. When the sun has set, and the moon has set, and the fire has gone out, and no sound is heard, what serves then as his light?

Yagnavalkya

The Self indeed is his light; for by the light of the Self man sits, moves about, does his work, and when his work is done, rests.

Janaka

Who is that Self?

Yagnavalkya

The self-luminous being who dwells within the

lotus of the heart, surrounded by the senses and
sense organs, and who is the light of the intellect,
is that Self. Becoming identified with the intellect,
he moves to and fro, through birth and death, between this world and the next. Becoming identified with the intellect, the Self appears to be thinking, appears to be moving. While the mind is
dreaming, the Self also appears to be dreaming,
and seems to be beyond the next world as well as
this.

When man, the individual soul, is born, and
assumes relationship with the body and sense organs, he becomes associated with the evils of the
world. When at death he gives up the body, he
leaves all evils behind.

There are two states for man—the state in this
world, and the state in the next; there is also a
third state, the state intermediate between these
two, which can be likened to dream. While in the
intermediate state, a man experiences both the
other states, that in this world and that in the
next; and the manner thereof is as follows: When
he dies, he lives only in the subtle body, on which
are left the impressions of his past deeds, and of
these impressions he is aware, illumined as they
are by the light of the Self. The pure light of the
Self affords him light. Thus it is that in the intermediate state he experiences the first state, or

that of life in the world. Again, while in the intermediate state, he foresees both the evils and the blessings that will yet come to him, as these are determined by his conduct, good and bad, upon the earth, and by the character in which this conduct has resulted. Thus it is that in the intermediate state he experiences the second state, or that of life in the world to come.

In the intermediate state, there are no real chariots, nor horses, nor roads; but by the light of the Self he creates chariots and horses and roads. There are no real blessings, nor joys, nor pleasures; but he creates blessings and joys and pleasures. There are no real ponds, nor lakes, nor rivers; but he creates ponds and lakes and rivers. He is the creator of all these out of the impressions left by his past deeds.

Regarding the different states of consciousness, it is written:

While one is in the state of dream, the golden, self-luminous being, the Self within, makes the body to sleep, though he himself remains forever awake and watches by his own light the impressions of deeds that have been left upon the mind. Thereafter, associating himself again with the consciousness of the organs of sense, the Self causes the body to awake.

While one is in the state of dream, the golden,

self-luminous being, the Self within, the Immortal One, keeps alive the house of flesh with the help of the vital force, but at the same time walks out of this house. The Eternal goes wherever he desires.

The self-luminous being assumes manifold forms, high and low, in the world of dreams. He seems to be enjoying the pleasure of love, or to be laughing with friends, or to be looking at terrifying spectacles.

Everyone is aware of the experiences; no one sees the Experiencer.

Some say that dreaming is but another form of waking, for what a man experiences while awake he experiences again in his dreams. Be that as it may, the Self, in dreams, shines by his own light.

Janaka

Revered sir, I offer you a thousand cattle. Instruct me further for the sake of my liberation.

Yagnavalkya

The Self, having in dreams tasted enjoyment, gone hither and thither, experienced both good and evil, attains to the state of dreamless sleep; then again he comes back to dreams. Whatever he may experience in dreams does not affect him, for the true nature of the Self remains forever unaffected.

Janaka

So it is indeed, Yagnavalkya. I offer you another thousand cattle, revered sir. Speak on for the
sake of my liberation.

Yagnavalkya

The Self, having in dreams tasted enjoyment,
gone hither and thither, experienced good and evil,
hastens back to the state of waking from which
he started. Whatever he may experience in dreams
does not affect him, for the true nature of the Self
remains forever unaffected.

Janaka

So it is indeed, Yagnavalkya. Another thousand
cattle shall be yours, revered sir. Speak on for the
sake of my liberation.

Yagnavalkya

The Self, having in wakefulness enjoyed the
pleasures of sense, gone hither and thither, experienced good and evil, hastens back again to his
dreams.

As a large fish moves from one bank of a river
to the other, so does the Self move between dreaming and waking.

As a hawk or a falcon flying in the sky becomes

tired, and stretching its wings comes back to its nest, so does the Self hasten to that state where, deep in sleep, he desires no more desires, and dreams no more dreams.

Indeed, the Self, in his true nature, is free from craving, free from evil, free from fear. As a man in the embrace of his loving wife knows nothing that is without, nothing that is within, so man in union with the Self knows nothing that is without, nothing that is within, for in that state all desires are satisfied. The Self is his only desire; he is free from craving, he goes beyond sorrow.

Then father is no father, mother is no mother; worlds disappear, gods disappear, scriptures disappear; the thief is no more, the murderer is no more, castes are no more; no more is there monk or hermit. The Self is then untouched either by good or by evil, and the sorrows of the heart are turned into joy.

He does not see, nor smell, nor taste, nor speak, nor hear, nor think, nor touch, nor know; for there is nothing separate from him, there is no second. Yet he can see, for sight and he are one; yet he can smell, for smelling and he are one; yet he can taste, for taste and he are one; yet he can speak, for speech and he are one; yet he can hear, for hearing and he are one; yet he can think, for thinking and he are one; yet he can touch, for touching and he are one; yet he can know, for knowing and he are one. Eternal is the light of consciousness; immortal is the Self.

When there is another, then one sees another, smells another, tastes another, speaks to another, hears another, thinks of another, touches and knows another.

Pure like crystal water is that Self, the only seer, the One without a second. He is the kingdom of Brahman, man's highest goal, his supreme treasure, his greatest bliss. Creatures who live within the bonds of ignorance experience but a small portion of his infinite being.

Janaka

You shall have still another thousand cattle. Speak on, revered sir, for the sake of my liberation.

Yagnavalkya

The Self, having in dreams enjoyed the pleasures of sense, gone hither and thither, experienced good and evil, hastens back to the state of waking from which he started.

As a man passes from dream to wakefulness, so does he pass at death from this life to the next.

When a man is about to die, the subtle body, mounted by the intelligent Self, groans—as a heavily laden cart groans under its burden.

When his body becomes thin through old age or disease, the dying man separates himself from his limbs, even as a mango or a fig or a banyan fruit separates itself from its stalk, and by the same way he came he hastens to his new abode, and there assumes another body, in which to begin a new life.

When his body grows weak and he becomes apparently unconscious, the dying man gathers his senses about him and completely withdrawing their powers descends into his heart. No more does he see form or color without.

He neither sees, nor smells, nor tastes. He does not speak, he does not hear. He does not think, he does not know. For all the organs, detaching themselves from his physical body, unite with his subtle body. Then the point of his heart, where the nerves join, is lighted by the light of the Self, and by that light he departs either through the eye, or through the gate of the skull, or through some other aperture of the body. When he thus departs, life departs; and when life departs, all the functions of the vital principle depart. The Self remains conscious, and, conscious, the dying man goes to his abode. The deeds of this life, and the impressions they leave behind, follow him.

As a leech, having reached the end of a blade of grass, takes hold of another blade and draws itself to it, so the Self, having left this body behind it unconscious, takes hold of another body and draws himself to it.

As a goldsmith, taking an old gold ornament, moulds it into another, newer and more beautiful, so the Self, having given up the body and left it unconscious, takes on a newer and better form, either that of the fathers, or that of the celestial singers, or that of the gods, or that of other beings, heavenly or earthly.

The Self is verily Brahman. Through ignorance it identifies itself with what is alien to it, and appears to consist of intellect, understanding, life, sight, hearing, earth, water, air, ether, fire, desire and the absence of desire, anger and the absence of anger, righteousness and the absence of righteousness. It appears to be all things—now one, now another.

As a man acts, so does he become. A man of good deeds becomes good, a man of evil deeds becomes evil. A man becomes pure through pure deeds, impure through impure deeds.

As a man's desire is, so is his destiny. For as his desire is, so is his will; as his will is, so is his deed; and as his deed is, so is his reward, whether good or bad.

A man acts according to the desires to which he clings. After death he goes to the next world, bear-

ing in his mind the subtle impressions of his deeds;
and after reaping there the harvest of his deeds, he
returns again to this world of action. Thus he who
has desire continues subject to rebirth.

But he in whom desire is stilled suffers no rebirth. After death, having attained to the highest,
desiring only the Self, he goes to no other world.
Realizing Brahman, he becomes Brahman.

When all the desires which once entered into
his heart have been driven out by divine knowledge, the mortal, attaining to Brahman, becomes
immortal.

As the slough of a snake lies cast off on an ant-
hill, so lies the body of a man at death; while he,
freed from the body, becomes one with the immortal spirit, Brahman, the Light Eternal.

Janako

Sir, again I give you a thousand cows. Speak
on, that I may be liberated.

Yagnavalkya

The path of liberation is subtle, and hard, and
long. I myself am walking in it; nay, I have
reached the end. By this path alone the wise, the
knowers of Brahman, having attained him while
living, achieve final liberation at death.

Other worlds there are, joyless, enveloped in

darkness. To these worlds, after death, go those who are unwise, who know not the Self.

When a man has realized the Self, the pure, the immortal, the blissful, what craving can be left in him that he should take to himself another body, full of suffering, to satisfy it?

He that has once known the glory of the Self within the ephemeral body—that stumbling-block to enlightenment—knows that the Self is one with Brahman, lord and creator of all.

Brahman may be realized while yet one dwells in the ephemeral body. To fail to realize him is to live in ignorance, and therefore to be subject to birth and death. The knowers of Brahman are immortal; others, knowing him not, continue in the bonds of grief.

He who with spiritual eye directly perceives the self-effulgent Being, the lord of all that was, is, and will be—he indeed is without fear, and causes fear in none.

He who knows Brahman to be the life of life, the eye of the eye, the ear of the ear, the mind of the mind—he indeed comprehends fully the cause of all causes.

By the purified mind alone is Brahman perceived.

In Brahman there is no diversity. He who sees diversity goes from death to death.

Brahman can be apprehended only as knowledge

itself—knowledge that is one with reality, inseparable from it. For he is beyond all proof, beyond all instruments of thought. The eternal Brahman is pure, unborn, subtler than the subtlest, greater than the greatest.

Let therefore the wise aspirant, knowing Brahman to be the supreme goal, so shape his life and his conduct that he may attain to him. Let him not seek to know him by arguments, for arguments are idle and vain.

Verily is Brahman the great unborn that dwells within the lotus of the heart, surrounded by the senses. He is the intellect of the intellect, protector of all, lord of all, king of all. Good works do not make him more, nor do evil works make him less. Lord, king, protector of all, he transcends the three worlds.

Devotees seek to know him by study, by sacrifice, by continence, by austerity, by detachment. To know him is to become a seer. Desiring to know him, and him alone, monks renounce the world. Realizing the glory of the Self, the sages of old craved not sons nor daughters. "What have we to do with sons and daughters," they asked, "we who have known the Self, we who have achieved the supreme goal of existence?" No longer desiring progeny, nor wealth, nor life in other worlds, they entered upon the path of complete renunciation.

Craving for progeny leads to craving for wealth, and craving for wealth leads to craving for life in other worlds. Two cravings there are: the craving for a life of pleasure in this world, and the craving for a life of greater pleasure in other worlds.

The Self is to be described as *not this, not that*. It is incomprehensible, for it cannot be comprehended; undecaying, for it does not decay; unattached, for it never attaches itself; unfettered, for it is never bound. He who knows the Self is unaffected, whether by good or by evil. Never do such thoughts come to him as "I have done an evil thing," or "I have done a good thing." Both good and evil he has transcended, and he is therefore troubled no more by what he may or may not have done.

The eternal glory of the knower of Brahman, beginningless and endless, revealed by divine knowledge, is neither increased nor decreased by deeds. Let a man therefore seek to find it, since having found it he can never be touched by evil. Self-controlled is he who knows the Self, tranquil, poised, free from desire. Absorbed in meditating upon it, he sees it within his own soul, and he sees all beings in it. Evil touches him not, troubles him not, for in the fire of his divine knowledge all evil is burnt away.

Freed from evil, freed from desire, freed from doubt, he becomes a knower of Brahman.

This, O King, is the truth of Brahman. Do thou attain to it!

Janaka

Most revered sir, I offer you the empire of Videha, and myself with it, to be your servant.

Yagnavalkya

The Self, the great unborn, the undecaying, the undying, the immortal, the fearless, is, in very truth, Brahman. He who knows Brahman is without fear. He who knows Brahman becomes Brahman!

Gods, men, and asuras—all three descendants of Prajapati—lived with him for a time as students.

Then the gods said: "Teach us, sir!" In reply Prajapati uttered one syllable: "Da." Then he said: "Have you understood?" They answered, "Yes, we have understood. You said to us, 'Damayata—Be self-controlled.' " "Yes," agreed Prajapati, "you have understood."

Then the men said: "Teach us, sir." Prajapati uttered the same syllable: "Da." Then he said:

"Have you understood?" They answered, "Yes, we have understood. You said to us, '*Datta*—Be charitable.' " "Yes," agreed Prajapati, "you have understood."

Then the asuras said: "Teach us, sir." Prajapati uttered the same syllable: "Da." Then he said: "Have you understood?" They said, "Yes, we have understood. You told us '*Da*yadhwam—Be compassionate.' " "Yes," agreed Prajapati, "you have understood."

The storm cloud thunders: "Da! Da! Da!—Be self-controlled! Be charitable! Be compassionate!"

XI

SWETASVATARA

MEDITATION can be learned, and it must be practiced according to accepted rules. By its means it is possible to realize the personal Brahman, who, in union with Maya, creates, preserves, and dissolves the universe, and likewise the impersonal Brahman, who transcends all forms of being, who eternally is, without attributes and without action.

SWETASVATARA

OM . . .
With our ears may we hear what is good.
With our eyes may we behold thy righteousness.
Tranquil in body, may we who worship thee find rest.
OM . . . Peace—peace—peace.
OM . . . Hail to the supreme Self!

Disciples inquire within themselves:

What is the cause of this universe?—is it Brahman? Whence do we come? Why do we live? Where shall we at last find rest? Under whose command are we bound by the law of happiness and its opposite?

Time, space, law, chance, matter, primal energy, intelligence—none of these, nor a combination of these, can be the final cause of the universe, for they also are effects, and exist to serve the soul. Nor can the individual self be the cause, for, being subject to the law of happiness and misery, it is not free.

The seers, absorbed in contemplation, saw within themselves the ultimate reality, the self-luminous being, the one God, who dwells as the self-conscious power in all creatures. He is One

without a second. Deep within all beings he
dwells, hidden from sight by the coverings of the
gunas—*sattwa, rajas,* and *tamas.* He presides over
time, space, and all apparent causes.

This vast universe is a wheel. Upon it are all
creatures that are subject to birth, death, and rebirth. Round and round it turns, and never stops.
It is the wheel of Brahman. As long as the individual self thinks it is separate from Brahman, it
revolves upon the wheel in bondage to the laws of
birth, death, and rebirth. But when through the
grace of Brahman it realizes its identity with him,
it revolves upon the wheel no longer. It achieves
immortality.[1]

He who is realized by transcending the world
of cause and effect, in deep contemplation, is ex-
pressly declared by the scriptures to be the Supreme
Brahman. He is the substance, all else the shadow.
He is the imperishable. The knowers of Brahman
know him as the one reality behind all that seems.
For this reason they are devoted to him. Absorbed
in him, they attain freedom from the wheel of
birth, death, and rebirth.

The Lord supports this universe, which is made
up of the perishable and the imperishable, the

---

[1] Here appears for the first time in extant Hindu litera-
ture the image of the wheel as applied to birth, death, and
rebirth.

manifest and the unmanifest. The individual soul, forgetful of the Lord, attaches itself to pleasure and thus is bound. When it comes to the Lord, it is freed from all its fetters.

Mind and matter, master and servant—both have existed from beginningless time. The Maya which unites them has also existed from beginningless time. When all three—mind, matter, and Maya—are known as one with Brahman, then is it realized that the Self is infinite and has no part in action. Then is it revealed that the Self is all.

Matter is perishable. The Lord, the destroyer of ignorance, is imperishable, immortal. He is the one God, the Lord of the perishable and of all souls. By meditating on him, by uniting oneself with him, by identifying oneself with him, one ceases to be ignorant.

Know God, and all fetters will be loosed. Ignorance will vanish. Birth, death, and rebirth will be no more. Meditate upon him and transcend physical consciousness. Thus will you reach union with the lord of the universe. Thus will you become identified with him who is One without a second. In him all your desires will find fulfillment.

The truth is that you are always united with the Lord. But you must *know* this. Nothing further is there to know. Meditate, and you will realize that mind, matter, and Maya (the power which unites mind and matter) are but three aspects of Brahman, the one reality.

Fire, though present in the firesticks, is not perceived until one stick is rubbed against another. The Self is like that fire: it is realized in the body by meditation on the sacred syllable OM.

Let your body be the stick that is rubbed, the sacred syllable OM the stick that is rubbed against it. Thus shall you realize God, who is hidden within the body as fire is hidden within the wood.

Like oil in sesame seeds, butter in cream, water in the river bed, fire in tinder, the Self dwells within the soul. Realize him through truthfulness and meditation.

Like butter in cream is the Self in everything. Knowledge of the Self is gained through meditation. The Self is Brahman. By Brahman is all ignorance destroyed.

To realize God, first control the outgoing senses and harness the mind. Then meditate upon the light in the heart of the fire—meditate, that is, upon pure consciousness as distinct from the ordinary consciousness of the intellect. Thus the Self, the Inner Reality, may be seen behind physical appearance.

Control your mind so that the Ultimate Reality,

the self-luminous Lord, may be revealed. Strive earnestly for eternal bliss.

With the help of the mind and the intellect, keep the senses from attaching themselves to objects of pleasure. They will then be purified by the light of the Inner Reality, and that light will be revealed.

The wise control their minds, and unite their hearts with the infinite, the omniscient, the all-pervading Lord. Only discriminating souls practice spiritual disciplines. Great is the glory of the self-luminous being, the Inner Reality.

Hear, all ye children of immortal bliss, also ye gods who dwell in the high heavens: Follow only in the footsteps of the illumined ones, and by continuous meditation merge both mind and intellect in the eternal Brahman. The glorious Lord will be revealed to you.

Control the vital force. Set fire to the Self within by the practice of meditation. Be drunk with the wine of divine love. Thus shall you reach perfection.

Be devoted to the eternal Brahman. Unite the light within you with the light of Brahman. Thus will the source of ignorance be destroyed, and you will rise above karma.

Sit upright, holding the chest, throat, and head erect. Turn the senses and the mind inward to the lotus of the heart. Meditate on Brahman with the help of the syllable OM. Cross the fearful currents of the ocean of worldliness by means of the raft of Brahman—the sacred syllable OM.

With earnest effort hold the senses in check. Controlling the breath, regulate the vital activities. As a charioteer holds back his restive horses, so does a persevering aspirant hold back his mind.

Retire to a solitary place, such as a mountain cave or any sacred spot. The place must be protected from the wind and rain, and it must have a smooth, clean floor, free from pebbles and dust. It must not be damp, and it must be free from disturbing noises. It must be pleasing to the eye and quieting to the mind. Seated there, practice meditation and other spiritual exercises.

As you practice meditation, you may see in vision forms resembling snow, crystal, wind, smoke, fire, lightning, fireflies, the sun, the moon. These are signs that you are on your way to the revelation of Brahman.

As you become absorbed in meditation, you will realize that the Self is separate from the body and for this reason will not be affected by disease, old age, or death.

The first signs of progress on the path of yoga are health, a sense of physical lightness, clearness of complexion, a beautiful voice, an agreeable odor of the person, and freedom from craving.

As a soiled piece of metal, when it has been cleaned, shines brightly, so the dweller in the body, when he has realized the truth of the Self, is freed from sorrow and attains to bliss.

The yogi experiences directly the truth of Brahman by realizing the light of the Self within. He is freed from all impurities—he the pure, the birthless, the bright.

He is the one God, present in the north, the east, the south, and the west. He is the creator. He enters into all wombs. He alone is now born as all beings, and he alone is to be born as all beings in the future. He is within all persons as the Inner Self, facing in all directions.

Let us adore the Lord, the bright one, who is in fire, who is in water, who is in plants and trees, who pervades the whole universe.

The one absolute, impersonal Existence, together with his inscrutable Maya, appears as the divine Lord, the personal God, endowed with manifold glories. With his divine power he holds dominion over all the worlds. At the periods of creation and dissolution of the universe, he alone exists. Those who realize him become immortal.

The Lord is One without a second. With his

divine power he rules over all the worlds. Within man he dwells, and within all other beings. He projects the universe, maintains it, and withdraws it into himself.

His eyes are everywhere; his face, his arms, his feet are in every place. Out of himself he has produced the heavens and the earth, and with his arms and his wings he holds them together.

He is the origin and support of the gods. He is the lord of all. He confers bliss and wisdom upon those who are devoted to him. He destroys their sins and their sorrows.

He punishes those who break his laws. He sees all and knows all. May he endow us with good thoughts!

O Lord, clothed in thy most holy form, which is calm and blissful, and which destroys all evil and ignorance, look upon us and make us glad.

O Lord, thou hast revealed thy sacred syllable OM, which is one with thee. In thy hands it is a weapon with which to destroy ignorance. O protector of thy devotees, do not conceal thy benign person.

Thou art the supreme Brahman. Thou art infinite. Thou hast assumed the forms of all creatures, remaining hidden in them. Thou pervadest all. Thou art the one God of the universe. Those who realize thee become immortal.

Said the great seer Swetasvatara:

I have known, beyond all darkness, that great Person of golden effulgence. Only by knowing him does one conquer death. There is no other way of escaping the wheel of birth, death, and rebirth.

There is nothing superior to him, nothing different from him, nothing subtler or greater than he. Alone he stands, changeless, self-luminous; he, the Great One, fills this universe.

Though he fills the universe, he transcends it. He is untouched by its miseries. He has no form. Those who know him become immortal. Others remain in the depths of misery.

The Lord God, all-pervading and omnipresent, dwells in the heart of all beings. Full of grace, he ultimately gives liberation to all creatures by turning their faces toward himself.

He is the innermost Self. He is the great Lord. He it is that reveals the purity within the heart by means of which he, who is pure being, may be reached. He is the ruler. He is the great Light, shining forever.

This great Being, assuming a form of the size of a thumb, forever dwells in the hearts of all creatures as their innermost Self. He can be known directly by the purified heart through spiritual discrimination. Knowing him, men become immortal.

This great Being has a thousand heads, a thousand eyes, and a thousand feet. He envelops the universe. Though transcendent, he is to be meditated upon as residing in the lotus of the heart, at the center of the body, ten fingers above the navel.

He alone is *all this*—what has been and what shall be. He has become this universe. Yet he remains forever changeless, and is the lord of immortality.

His hands and feet are everywhere; his eyes, heads, and mouths are everywhere. His ears are everywhere. He pervades everything in the universe.

Without organs of sense, yet reflecting the activities of the senses, he is the lord and ruler of all.

He is the friend and refuge of all.

He resides in the body, the city of nine gates. He sports in the world without in innumerable forms. He is the master, the ruler, of the whole world, animate and inanimate.

He moves fast, though without feet. He grasps everything, though without hands. He sees all, though without eyes. He hears everything, though without ears. He knows all, but none knows him. He is called the Supreme, the Great One.

Subtler than the subtlest, greater than the greatest, the Self is hidden in the heart of all creatures. Through his grace a man loses his cravings, transcends grief, and realizes him as Brahman Supreme.

O Brahman Supreme!
Formless art thou, and yet
(Though the reason none knows)
Thou bringest forth many forms;
Thou bringest them forth, and then
Withdrawest them to thyself.
Fill us with thoughts of thee!

Thou art the fire,
Thou art the sun,
Thou art the air,
Thou art the moon,
Thou art the starry firmament,
Thou art Brahman Supreme:
Thou art the waters—thou,
The creator of all!

Thou art woman, thou art man,
Thou art the youth, thou art the maiden,
Thou art the old man tottering with his staff;
Thou facest everywhere.

Thou art the dark butterfly,
Thou art the green parrot with red eyes,
Thou art the thunder cloud, the seasons, the seas.
Without beginning art thou,
Beyond time, beyond space.

Thou art he from whom sprang
The three worlds.

Maya is thy divine consort—
Wedded to thee.
Thou art her master, her ruler.
Red, white, and black is she,
Each color a guna.
Many are her children—
The rivers, the mountains,
Flower, stone, and tree,
Beast, bird, and man—
In every way like herself.
Thou, spirit in flesh,
Forgetting what thou art,
Unitest with Maya—
But only for a season.
Parting from her at last,
Thou regainest thyself.

Thou, Brahman Immortal,
And thou, woven of clay
(Two beings, yet one)—
Like two beautiful birds,
Golden of plumage,
Companions inseparable,
Perched high up on the branches
Of the selfsame tree—

As man thou tastest
The sweet fruits of the tree,
The sweet and bitter fruits:
But as Brahman, master of Maya,
Thou remainest unseen,
Immobile,
Calmly observing.

Forgetting his oneness with thee,
Bewildered by his weakness,
Full of sorrow is man;
But let him look close on thee,
Know thee as himself,
O Lord, most worshipful,
And behold thy glory—
Lo, all his heavy sorrow
Is turned to joy.

Changeless thou art,
Supreme, pure!
In thee dwell the gods.
The source of all scriptures thou art:
Yet what shall scriptures avail
If they be smooth on the lip,
But absent from the heart?
To him who knows thee comes fullness—
To him alone!

Thou art lord and master of Maya,
Man is her slave.
With Maya uniting, thou hast brought forth the
     universe.
The source of all scriptures thou art,
And the source of all creeds.
The universe is thy Maya;
And thou, great God, her lord,
Wherever the eye falls,
There, within every form,
Thou dwellest.

One thou art, one only.
Born from many wombs,
Thou hast become many:
Unto thee all return.
Thou, Lord God, bestowest all blessings,
Thou the Light, thou the Adorable One.
Whoever finds thee
Finds infinite peace.

Thou art Lord God of all gods,
All the worlds rest in thee;
Thou art ruler of the beasts,
Two-footed, four-footed;
Our heart's worship be thine!
Thou art the blissful Lord,

Subtler than the subtlest.
In thee alone is there peace.

Thou, sole guardian of the universe,
Thou, lord of all,
In the hearts of thy creatures
Thou hidest thyself.
Gods and seers become one with thee.
Those who know thee die not.

Of all religions thou art the source.
The light of thy knowledge shining,
There is nor day nor night,
Nor being nor non-being—
Thou alone art.

Thou alone art—thou the Light
Imperishable, adorable;
Great Glory is thy name.
No one is there beside thee,
No one equal to thee.

Invisible is thy form,
Invisible to mortal eyes;
The seers alone
In their purified hearts—
They alone see thee.
They alone are immortal.

Neither male nor female art thou,
Nor neuter;
Whatsoever form thou assumest,
That thou art.

Thou dost pervade the universe,
Thou art consciousness itself,
Thou art creator of time.
All-knowing art thou.
At thy bidding Maya,
Thy power divine,
Projects this visible universe,
Projects name and form.

Thou art the Primal Being.
Thou appearest as this universe
Of illusion and dream.
Thou art beyond time.
Indivisible, infinite, the Adorable One—
Let a man meditate on thee
Within his heart,
Let him consecrate himself to thee,
And thou, infinite Lord,
Wilt make thyself known to him.

Thou, womb and tomb of the universe,
And its abode;
Thou, source of all virtue,

Destroyer of all sins—
Thou art seated in the heart.
When thou art seen,
Time and form disappear.
Let a man feel thy presence,
Let him behold thee within,
And to him shall come peace,
Eternal peace—
To none else, to none else!

Thou art the eternal among non-eternals,
The consciousness of the conscious;
Though one, thou fulfillest
The desires of many.

Let a man devote himself
To knowledge of thee,
Let him follow thy path,
And he shall know thee:
All his fetters shall be loosed.

Can a man roll up the sky
Like a piece of skin?
Can he end his misery
And know not thee?

If the truths of these scriptures are meditated upon by a man in the highest degree devoted to God, and to his Guru as to his God, they will shine forth. They will shine forth indeed!

OM . . . Peace—peace—peace.

XII

KAIVALYA

THE sage who by faith, devotion, and meditation has realized the Self and become one with Brahman, is released from the wheel of change and escapes from rebirth, sorrow, and death.

KAIVALYA

May Brahman protect us,
May he guide us,
May he give us strength and right understanding.
May love and harmony be with us all.
OM . . . Peace—peace—peace.

Disciple

MASTER, teach me the knowledge of Brahman.
I hear that this is the supreme knowledge, hidden
and sacred, sought by the wise, and that he who
seeks it is freed from impurities and attains the
Supreme Being.

Teacher

Seek to know Brahman by acquiring faith in
the word of the scriptures and in your Guru. Be
devoted to Brahman. Meditate on him unceasingly.
Not by work, nor by progeny, nor by wealth, but
by devotion to him and by indifference to the
world, does a man reach immortality.

The supreme heaven shines in the lotus of the
heart. They enter there who struggle and aspire.

Understanding the spirit of the scriptural teachings, they renounce the world.

Retire into solitude. Seat yourself on a clean spot and in erect posture, with the head and neck in a straight line. Be indifferent to the world. Control all the sense organs. Bow down in devotion to your Guru. Then enter the lotus of the heart and there meditate on the presence of Brahman— the pure, the infinite, the blissful.

Unmanifest to the senses, beyond all thought, infinite in form, is God. He is the doer of all good; he is forever tranquil; he is immortal. He is One, without beginning, middle, or end; he is all-pervading. He is infinite wisdom, and he is bliss.

The seers meditate on him and reach the source of all beings, the witness of all. He goes beyond all darkness. He is Brahma, he is Shiva, he is Indra, he is the supreme, the changeless Reality. He is Vishnu, he is the primal energy, he is eternity. He is all. He is what has been and what shall be. He is eternal. He who knows him conquers death. There is no other way to liberation.

By seeing the Self in all beings, and all beings in the Self, one goes to Brahman. That is the only way.

The mind may be compared to a firestick, the syllable OM to another. Rub the two sticks together by repeating the sacred word and meditating on Brahman, and the flame of knowledge will be kindled in your heart and all impurities will be burnt away.

He, as the Self, resides in all forms, but is veiled by ignorance. When he is in the state of dream that men call waking, he becomes the individual self, and enjoys food, drink, and many other pleasures. When he is in the state of dream that men call dreaming, he is happy or miserable because of the creations of his mind. And when he is in the state of dream that men call dreamless sleep, he is overcome by darkness, he experiences nothing, he enjoys rest.

At death he is born again, and the circumstances of his new life are determined by his past deeds and by the habits he has formed. He continues to live in the three states of consciousness—waking, dreaming, and dreamless sleep. As long as he continues in these states, he is the individual self. He, as the Self, is infinite, indivisible; he is consciousness, bliss. In him are merged all the three states of consciousness. From him are born mind, life, and the senses; earth, air, water, fire, and ether. He is the reality behind all existence.

He is the Supreme Brahman. He is in all, he is the foundation of all. Subtler than the subtlest is he. He is eternal. Thou art he! Thou art he!

He who made this great spectacle of waking,

dream, and dreamless sleep—he I am. I am Brahman: know this, and break all bonds.

In the three states of consciousness, whatever appears as the enjoyer or the object of enjoyment, I am the witness thereof, separate from all. I am pure consciousness. I am the eternal Shiva.

From me all emerge, in me all exist, and to me all return. I am Brahman—One without a second.

I am subtler than the subtlest; I am greater than the greatest; I am the Eternal Being. I am this manifold universe. I am the Lord of golden effulgence. I am Shiva.

I am without hands or feet. My divine powers none can conceive. I see, though without eyes. I hear, though without ears. I know all, but none knows me. I am infinite wisdom. I am the One to be known through the scriptures. I am the knower of all scriptures. Merit or demerit does not affect me. I was not born; I have neither body, nor senses, nor mind. I, the Supreme Self, dwell in the lotus of the heart. I am pure. I am One without a second.

OM . . . Peace—peace—peace.